MEDITATION
IN CHRISTIANITY

MEDITATION IN CHRISTIANITY

Swami Rama
Rev. Lawrence Bouldin/Justin O'Brien, D.Th./Father William Teska
Arpita, Ph.D./Sister Francis Borgia Rothluebber
Pandit Usharbudh Arya, D.Litt.

The Himalayan International Institute
of Yoga Science and Philosophy of the U.S.A.
Honesdale, Pennsylvania

Cover Illustration: *Variation within a Sphere, No. 10: The Sun* by Richard Lippold. The Metropolitan Museum of Art, Fletcher Fund, 1956. [56.106]. Reprinted by permission.

Library of Congress Cataloging in Publication Data
Meditation in Christianity.
    1. Meditation—Addresses, essays, lectures. 2. Yoga—Addresses, essays, lectures. I. Rama, Swami, 1925-   . II. Himalayan International Institute of Yoga Science and Philosophy.
BV4813.M4 1983   248.3'4   83-32
ISBN 0-89389-085-5

Revised and Enlarged Edition. First Printing 1983
Second Printing 1984

Contents

Introduction

From the beginnings of Christianity (and even earlier in the religious life of the people of Israel) there has been a tradition of meditation that persists to this day. It is the purpose of the present volume to explore this tradition.

Our reasons for selecting the articles to be included have been fourfold: First, we have attempted to present a view of the relationship of Christianity to other Eastern traditions in which there is a dominant emphasis on meditation. Historical evidence is presented, for instance, that points to the likelihood that Jesus and the fathers of the Christian faith were well acquainted with the ancient meditative disciplines. It is also shown how the purpose of meditation in Christianity became less important as the various modes of worship and dogma replaced the experiential knowledge of meditation as the basis of Christian belief.

A second intent of this volume is to examine the basis for meditation within the Bible itself. There has been a continuous, though often suppressed, tradition within the church that has found in the scriptures an esoteric guide to the practice of meditation as well as a source of hidden wisdom that becomes more fully apparent to aspirants as they progress along the spiritual path. This wellspring of spiritual truth has always nourished the great mystics and teachers of Christianity. It remains today the chief resource for persons who are seeking to unfold within themselves a greater awareness of the indwelling consciousness of Christ.

A third reason for this volume is to trace the history of a significant meditative tradition within the church—a tradition that has spanned many centuries. From this, much can be learned that will be of help to all who seek to establish a method of meditation based on Christian insights and goals.

And, finally, the present volume includes a discussion of some of the obstacles that stand in the way of successful meditation. Some of these are personal and require a change in the style and values of one's life; others are rooted in the narrowness of sectarianism and dogmatism in religion. But whatever the reason for them, as the hindrances to meditation are cleared away, one will find the key that frees him from the bondage of ignorance and attachments of the world, and it then becomes possible for him to experience the "new birth" of an expanded capacity to perceive and respond to the infinite consciousness which is God.

Meditation thus gives us hope for a future of peace on earth and for the attainment of brotherhood among men, for through meditation one rediscovers the essential unity of purpose that underlies the many approaches to realization of God.

Lawrence M. Bouldin

Meditation in Christianity

Swami Rama

Religion should not consist of mere intellectual conformity. The human mind is badly crippled by thinking that truth has already been found and that nothing remains for us except to reproduce the same beliefs over and over. Religion is the fulfillment of life; it is an experience in which every aspect of being is raised to its highest state. What is needed to attain this, however, is not dogma; it is a change of consciousness, a rebirth, an inner revolution. There is no such thing as the automatic evolution of humanity; evolution is possible only through conscious effort. As they are, human beings remain unfinished beings. They must seek their own completion. People have to grow into regenerate beings and allow the Christ consciousness to flow through them. This is the teaching of Christianity.

Jesus asks us to bring about this rebirth, but it can take place only through higher knowledge and meditation, not through external living habits or vocal prayer alone. When Jesus rebukes the Pharisees, for instance, he is condemning the man of pretenses who keeps up appearances. "Except your righteousness shall exceed the righteousness of the scribes and Pharisees," he said, "ye shall in no wise enter the kingdom of Heaven" (Matt. 5:20). In other words, to attain heaven (which is the higher level of understanding) one has to grow, and this comes about through prayer, purity, self-control, studying life, and meditation. Christ and Buddha, for instance, freed themselves from the restricting notions of orthodox traditions, and that is the reason they could spread the universal gospel of truth, love, and service.

Jesus says of John the Baptist that he is the best of those born

3

of women but that the least of the kingdom of heaven was greater than he. For example, John speaks to us of salvation through moral life; he tells us what to do, but he does not tell us how to be. Jesus insists on inner transformation. John asks us to become better; Jesus asks us to become new. John the Baptist was puzzled when he heard that Jesus and His disciples drank wine and did not fast. He could not understand it when they plucked the ears of corn on the Sabbath day or when Jesus healed on the Sabbath. John is still a man born of woman; he has not experienced rebirth. Jesus tells us, "Except a man be born again he cannot see the kingdom of God" (John 3:3), and Paul says, "Awake, thou that sleepest and arise from the dead" (Eph. 5:14). Originally, Christian teachings—before they became externalized and dogmatized— focused on awakening from sleep through the light shed by inner wisdom. Jesus Christ was one who had done this and who taught others the way.

Religion is not theology, and it is not magic or witchcraft. It should not spoil the simplicity of truth. Religion is not limited to the data of perception or introspection; it is an experience to be lived, not a theory or belief to be accepted. When a person surrounds his soul with a shell, such as national pride or the empty presumptions of dogma, he suppresses the breath of the spirit. Christianity, on the other hand, is a liberating power that is based on the life and experience of Jesus. The cross becomes significant when we make it our own and undergo crucifixion. Only then can we experience rebirth. "Seek and you shall find" (Matt. 7:7), said Jesus, but each of us must seek independently. The truth that is latent in every soul must become manifest. Then shall we be able to work in newness of life. "Marvel not that I have said unto thee, 'Ye must be born again'" (John 3:7). In this spirit, says St. Paul, ". . . Know ye not that ye are the temple of God and that the spirit of God dwelleth in you? . . . You are the temple of the living God" (1 Cor. 3:16-17). One who enters inwardly penetrates intimately into himself and, going beyond self, becomes perfect.

In early Christianity meditation was practiced in all the

monasteries, and the cross, a symbol for physical suffering, mortification, and earthly defeat, was also a symbol for spiritual victory. Through suffering lies the way of liberation. Pascal says that Jesus struggles with death until the end of the world, and in this boundless Gethsemane that is the universe, we have to struggle on unto death, wherever a tear falls, wherever a heart is seized with despair, wherever an injustice or an act of violence is committed. "Hast thou seen thy brother, then thou hast seen God." This, the motto of the early Christians, is just as valid to us today.

The Christian Tradition of Meditation

Scriptural witness to meditation pervades both the Old Testament and the Gospels. For instance, in the Psalms one reads:

> Let the words of my mouth and the meditation of my heart be acceptable in thy sight, O Lord, my rock and my redeemer. (Psalm 19:14)
>
> Be still, and know that I am God. (Psalm 46:10)
>
> Let me hear what God the Lord will speak . . . to those who turn to him in their hearts. (Psalm 85:8)
>
> I commune with my heart in the night; I meditate and search my spirit. (Psalm 77:6)
>
> May my meditation be pleasing to him, for I rejoice in the Lord. (Psalm 104:34)
>
> On the glorious splendor of thy majesty, and on thy wondrous works, I will meditate. (Psalm 145:5)

Further witness of meditation in Christianity can be found in the New Testament, which frequently shows Jesus retiring from the crowds to be alone in meditation, urging his followers to seek the "Father" within. Furthermore, St. Paul's Epistles describe the process of unfolding and inner transformation as one progresses on the path of Christ consciousness. These are but a few instances, among hundreds in the Bible, that clearly reflect the inner experiences of the higher nature. Somewhere, however, the thread between early and modern Christianity was broken—especially regarding the tradition of meditation—and that is the reason why the modern Christian does not receive initiation in meditation. It is also one of the reasons why many people are dissatisfied with the Christian religion as it is known today. Its practical aspect—meditation—is missing.

Meditation is the means for developing the inner life, and this has been reaffirmed by the acknowledged mystics of Christianity. For example:

> Our meditation in this present life should be in the praise of God; for the external exultation of our life hereafter will be the praise of God: and none can become fit for the future life who hath not practiced himself for it now. (St. Augustine)

> Let me know myself, Lord, and I shall know Thee. (St. Augustine)

> No one can be saved without self-knowledge. (St. Bernard)

> Let us enter the cell of self-knowledge. (St. Catherine of Siena)

The above quotations, if deeply studied and properly understood, reveal that in the long line of Christian sages the practice of meditation was more essential than verbal prayer.

Many admirers of Christian mysticism may acknowledge the testimony of mystics but characterize these individuals as exceptional, their experiences beyond the potential of modern seekers. This pessimism endures because Western Christians are not aware of an overlooked tradition, one in which meditation was taught widely. The meditative tradition at one time dominated early Christianity in the Middle East. After studying the history of the early Christians and the Desert Fathers, we know that they meditated day and night, and that meditation was not a new concept for them. Regardless of whether Abba, Paul, or St. Anthony was the first monk and father of the desert, it is quite certain that St. Anthony established a school of very systematic meditation in A.D. 310. It was situated on a mountain, called St. Anthony, sixty-five miles south of Cairo, and there he guided thousands of monks on the path of meditation. Another monastery, the monastery of Tabenna in upper Egypt, was founded by Paul in A.D. 300. According to historical data, Paul was born a few years before the close of the third century, and later in his life he guided monks in practices similar to those of the school of St. Anthony. His school also endorsed the practice of silence.

In all, there were about five thousand monks practicing meditation and austerity in the Desert of Nitra, or the Nitron Valley, in Egypt around that time, and during the second half of the fourth century a large number of ascetics lived all around Cairo. Christianity began to replace the myths and gods of Egypt, and the sign of the cross was often seen instead of the ancient symbols.

To further trace the history of meditation in the West, it is mentioned in various scriptures that two monks from India accompanied Alexander the Great to the Middle East and established a school of meditation in the general region where Anthony and Paul had founded their monasteries. History shows that early Eastern Christianity had a long line of sages, competent in the art of meditation, and comparative studies reveal that their ascetic practices were very similar to, or the same as, those practiced by Indian monks and sages. There is no doubt in my mind that the fathers of the desert and of Mt. Athos, as well as St. Anthony, knew the methods of meditation. This was also the time when Patanjali's school of meditation was influencing the various sects and religions of the Far East and Middle East. Unfortunately, Western Christianity has never seriously absorbed this genuine meditative tradition.

It is also interesting to note that yogic breathing was practiced in the fifth century A.D. by the Hesychast monks. In addition, the spiritual writings of the Hesychastic period teach that the human body has certain focal points that correspond to the *chakras* of yoga—the navel, the heart, the throat, and the mid-brow. The Hesychast monks, like the yogis, would concentrate upon these points in conjunction with rhythmic breathing and prayerful words, and by learning to control the respiration, the aspirant reached a tranquil state and tasted previously unknown spiritual experiences. According to the Hesychasts and the yogis, a transformation of character was gradually produced as one progressed in the art of meditative breathing and the accompanying necessary ascetic practices. Disruptive feelings, ill thoughts, and uncontrollable actions were gradually tranquilized by the steady practice of holy breathing (yogic breathing).

Later, during the Middle Ages, the confluence of Hesychastic prayer and meditation continued to prevail in Christian monasteries, and the great Byzantine mystic St. Simeon (949-1022), practiced and taught these methods of meditation (see *Orientalia Christiana*). One also finds the theory of breathing and the mystic physiology (called *sushumna dhyanam* in yogic manuals) in some modern spiritual treatises that relate breathing to various meditative states.

In addition, two orders who claim to have their own unbroken traditions—the Rosicrucians and the Freemasons—provide us with evidence to suggest a similar connection with yoga. These two orders are very close and often work together, and one finds in their esoteric and mystical histories living testimonials to the fact that they used the symbol for what the yogis consider to be the mother sound, *OM*. For reference one can go through lectures on Masonic symbolism written by the late Grand Master Albert Pike, who explains that *OM* was converted into Egyptian symbols:

> Coleman (*Mythology of the Hindus*) says that Om is a mystic symbol signifying the supreme God of Gods, which the Hindus, from its lawful and sacred meaning, hesitate to pronounce aloud, and in doing so place one of their hands before their mouths. . . .

Understanding the Path of Meditation

The systematic practice of meditation within a definite and accepted metaphysical framework is congenial to all religious schools of the world, for their goal is the same—to bring the aspirants to the highest state of consciousness. Without sufficient understanding of how and why meditation should be practiced, the meditative process cannot lead to this highest state, but if the process is properly understood on all levels, there will be inner peace and a unique experience of profound harmony along the way. In attempting to achieve this meditative experience, however, the aspirant is sooner or later threatened by two restrictions. The first is that the aspirant naturally tends to remain within the traditional boundaries of his accepted metaphysical and religious beliefs. This is the biggest obstacle. The second restriction is that the orthodox methods of meditation prescribed by Hindus, Buddhists, Jews, or Christians discourage people from moving outside their own meditative approach.

Every theological system requires its followers to believe in a definite way, with definite notions of God, soul, heaven, hell, sin, and virtue. But any pre-determined notions that one carries to the deeper states of meditation binds the meditator and prevents him from crossing the boundaries of the conditioned mind. One can receive higher experiences from this kind of meditation, but they are limited. Consequently, when one is restricted by dogma, one cannot realize the universal truth that the Self within is the Self of all. This enlightenment remains far away from the vision of such a meditator.

To tread the path of enlightenment, it is therefore important for the meditator to fully understand a few terms that are often confusing. The first concept is that of evil. Theologians have argued for ages over the problem of evil. Why does it exist? Why are people not aware of truth? These questions have been answered by the rare and gifted ones who have transcended human consciousness, with its belief in good and evil. For those who are on the plane of relative consciousness, the problem of how evil exists arises through academic and theological concepts, but saints and sages who have attained Christ consciousness tell us that evil does not exist at all. They say that we need only to know how to remove our ignorance to find that evil resides only in our sense of ego. Ego veils our eyes, and ignorance results. In reality, we are spirit. We have body, senses, and mind, but when we forget that we are spirit and identify ourselves with the body, senses, and mind, the sense of ego intervenes, and we forget our super-conscious nature. Thus, by living on the sense plane, we become subject to believing in the devil, for with our consciousness fragmented by the attractions of the sense level, we fail to understand the incompatibility of affirming the existence of both God and the devil.

So ego is the second concept one must understand, and whether one is Hindu, Buddhist, or Christian the problem of life amounts to this: How can one get rid of the ego? The answer given by the great sages of all religions is one and the same: Surrender yourself to God, and love God with all your heart, mind, and soul; let individual consciousness be absorbed by God consciousness. It sounds so simple to get rid of the ego, but it is the most difficult thing one can possibly do. If right discipline, patience, and perseverance are practiced, it is possible. But the mind's tendencies toward the pleasant are usually stronger than its tendencies toward the good, and the ego perpetually reasserts itself. Continuous sincere effort is therefore the only way to get rid of it.

The third concept is belief. We often console ourselves with the thought that God is sufficient for enlightenment, but unless there is a clear conception of what this means, unfoldment cannot occur. Distorted beliefs halt growth; knowledge alone dispels the darkness of ignorance. Believing in God is a positive help, but enlightenment is not possible without direct experience. No freedom is possible through mere belief—in order to gain freedom, one must have an earnest desire to attain higher knowledge.

A one-pointed mind is essential to God realization. We should approach truth through one way only. If one practices meditation in one way today and another tomorrow, for instance, it does not make the mind one-pointed. Some teachers give their students many different objects to meditate upon, but this does not help the mind to become steady. Unless there is only one chosen ideal or object to love or meditate upon, there cannot be any progress. Single-minded devotion toward one's ideal is very important. If one's ideal is Christ, then it is helpful to know that this same ideal is the absolute unmanifested One who is meditated upon by others in various names and forms. The Christ is your soul, and you should learn to see him in all beings, to feel and know that he is your shepherd and treasure. You should awaken the faculty of spiritual discrimination to know the difference between the real and the unreal. Then you will know that Christ is the abiding Reality and that all else is merely appearance. With such knowledge, liberation is possible, but it should be combined with earnest desire, sincere effort, and spiritual discipline. Otherwise, progress is impossible.

Prayer is the fourth concept to be understood. It is communication between the lower and higher domains, and it often takes the shape of a petition. Many people mistake prayer for meditation, which is the continuation of one thought. In meditation, individual interests are transcended by a one-pointed mind that desires to fathom the desireless and unfathomable realms of life. There is a further difference between petitionary prayer and meditation: in petitionary prayer there is always a demand for something, but in meditation one transcends the thinking process and all conditioning of the mind. Prayer is also different from contemplation, in which one ponders certain ideals. Prayer and contemplation are dualistic, but in meditation, when the final state has been reached, there is a direct "yoking" of the soul with God, and a monistic state is realized. All metaphysical and religious laws are left behind when one reaches this highest state of unity, and only meditation expands individual consciousness to universal Christ consciousness.

The Unfoldment of Meditation

The word *meditation* is used in various ways, but however it is used, it always refers to techniques that deal with one's inner nature. Through these techniques one finally transcends all levels of the mind and goes on to Christ consciousness and realization of the absolute One. Meditation does not require a belief in dogma or in any authority. It is an inward journey in which one studies one's own self on all levels, and ultimately reaches the source of consciousness. The aim of meditation is Self-realization—a direct vision of Truth. It is not an intellectual pursuit, nor is it emotional rapture. One's whole being is involved. It is neither suppression, which makes one passive, nor is it the acquisition of any experience that is not already within us. Meditation leads one from want to wantlessness. It is a way of going from the known to the unknown. The process can hardly be explained by words, but it leads one from the personal, through the transpersonal, and finally unites one with the highest One. It transforms the whole personality.

Life is a series of experiences, but all experiences do not lead us and become guides in the path of unfoldment. There are experiences, however, that great sages have witnessed from the deeper realms of their being—experiences that do not come from the contact of the senses with sense objects. The sages talk of the bliss that proceeds from the inner depths of the self, the eternal spring of bliss that lies within the heart of man. Realization of this bliss brings life-fulfillment and wisdom. Like the kingdom of heaven in the parable of Jesus, it is found not in some place remote from life, but within life itself:

> And when he was demanded of the Pharisees, when the kingdom of God should come, he answered them and said, The kingdom of God cometh not with observation. Neither shall they say, Lo, here! or, Lo, there! for, behold, the kingdom of God is within you. (Luke 17:20-21)

By what means can such an experience be obtained? Frequently, Western Christians condemn the philosophy of meditation, but it is actually the heart of Christianity. Yoking with God, or Christ consciousness, cannot be realized by merely reciting the verses of the Bible or the sayings of Christ.

> Man, if thou wishest to know what it is to pray ceaselessly: Enter into thyself, and interrogate the Spirit of God. (Angelus Silesius Cherub 1:237)

Jesus expresses this truth in the New Testament:

> Ask, and it shall be given unto you; seek and ye shall find; knock, and it shall be opened unto you. For every one that asketh, receiveth; and he that seeketh, findeth; and to him that knocketh, it shall be opened. (Matt. 7:7-8)

> And when thou prayest, thou shalt not be as the hypocrites are: for they love to pray standing in the synagogues and in the corners of the streets, that they may be seen of men. Verily I say unto you, they have their reward. But thou, when thou prayest, enter into thy closet, and when thou has shut thy door, pray to thy Father, which is in secret; and thy Father which seeth in secret shall reward thee openly. (Matt. 6:5-6)

Jesus said, "Seek and ye shall find," but how do we realize this truth? When one forgets his true nature, that "kingdom of God within," he loses his way in the tangle of the world. Who will show him the way back to what he has forgotten? Only he himself can do this. The purer the mind, the more easily it is controlled and disciplined, and a pure, disciplined mind finds its way to God. The whole process of spiritual and ethical discipline leads one to the awareness of the reality existing behind personality and nature. Through the senses one becomes aware of differences, but through Christ consciousness one becomes aware of the unity that is behind these differences. Just as ethics discovers laws that link the different aspects of sense experience, the philosophy of meditation unravels the laws of yoking the individual with the ultimate One.

Meditation is a search within oneself on various levels that finally leads one to that center from whence consciousness flows. A proper method of meditation helps one to discover the ultimate unifying principle of the universe. When methods for spiritual growth are properly understood and rightly practiced they will guide one toward the only way of transcending the self and going to the superconscious state.

In other words, when one is moved by the deeper problems and starts questioning oneself, mere promises in the scriptures are not satisfying. When one realizes the importance of life and its purpose, then one turns to the philosophy of meditation and finds the solutions therein. Patanjali, for instance, in the Yoga Sutras, outlines a systematic and detailed training program that is free of religious bias. The millions of people in both the East and the West who are genuinely interested in meditation can follow his guidelines regardless of their religion.

The Process of Meditation

From the very beginning, meditation requires a seeking, questioning, and logical mind, aided by the help of the right method. In addition, the seeker must perform actions selflessly, with love, one-pointedness, self-purity, and righteousness. Otherwise, the yoking of the mind is not possible. Thus can meditation, in its creative and dynamic aspects, be practiced. But first one must develop the right spiritual attitude through performing selfless action in the external world. This is called meditation in action. Another method of meditation is to sit in a calm and quiet place, on a firm seat, in a relaxed and comfortable posture, and then become aware of the breath and make the mind one-pointed by allowing it to attend to the flow of breath. When the mind has become concentrated, the *mantra* (a sound or word to make the mind one-pointed) given for meditation should be remembered. Constant remembrance of the mantra leads the student to a higher state of mind, and such a mind is capable of going beyond its limitations. Finally, when the mind goes beyond the dimensions of its own created conditions, there dawns Christ consciousness.

This second type of meditation has been practiced by yogis and monks who have devoted their whole lives to realizing the Truth. First, they withdraw their sense awareness from the objects of the world and their physical selves. Second, they concentrate the mind on a mantra, and then, when the mind starts flowing like a stream of oil, it becomes one-pointed and can transcend the limitations of emotional and rational boundaries. Thus new habits are formed and old habits are cast off. This is called spiritual rebirth. In other words, when the mind constantly thinks of God, meditation becomes a constant remembrance, and it flows like an unbroken stream. In such a case there cannot be any bondage. Constant recollection and ceaseless prayer become a means to liberation, and meditation becomes constant remembering. So in order to have an unbroken memory of God, one should meditate regularly. The mind should flow unceasingly toward God within. Then, when one constantly lives, moves, and has his being in God, the body becomes a temple.

Theology says that God exists and that we should believe in Him. Philosophy says that we should know the relationship between the individual, the universe, and the Creator. Meditation gives a direct vision of God in the temple of the body. A meditator does not have to search, roam, or wander in pursuit of God; a meditator finds the beloved within. The foolish person keeps searching on the sense plane, for all the distractions are at the outer gate of the temple. But when one enters into the inner chamber, shutting the outer gate, one finds his majesty, the center of Christ consciousness. Then one is reborn and becomes a free citizen of the kingdom of God. Such a person becomes universal. The practice of love is the natural awareness of God, and those who are constantly aware of the reality of the Lord within become the beloved of the Lord. They alone gain liberation; they receive direction and can guide others.

Thus, to be perfect and to attain the kingdom of heaven is the attainable goal of humankind. It is within us all. We stand midway between the visible and invisible worlds—but to get to the inner experience we must abstract ourselves from the outer. It should be remembered that all great religions teach the same fundamental truth, but that the great messengers of this truth tear down traditional values and establish a new order, according to the needs of their times. That is what Erasmus meant when he delivered the great dictum, "Wherever you encounter truth, look upon it as Christianity." By transcending national, religious, and traditional boundaries, meditation transforms an individual into a cosmic person. The result of meditation is therefore revolution, for it brings about the transformation of the personality of the meditator. False values are left behind and new values are established. Thus starts reformation in the world.

Meditation in the Bible

Rev. Lawrence Bouldin

The essence of religion is to awaken us to a full awareness of that great center of peace, wisdom, and freedom that lies veiled in the self within us. "Seek first the kingdom of God," taught the master, Jesus, stressing that one's primary duty in life is to seek an unfolding consciousness of our unity with God within and without. The purpose of the scriptures is to assist in this, the basic mission of human life, by continually directing those who aspire to eternal truth to seek ever higher levels of spiritual awareness.

Scriptures are read and studied by those who are at quite different stages in their development of spiritual awareness, and what can be understood by some remains shrouded in darkness for others. What is a key to advancement for one may be read with little appreciation by another. Still, it is a basic tenet of the ancient tradition that the deeper levels of meaning in the scriptures will be revealed to persons who are ready to understand them, and to his inner circle of disciples Jesus revealed the hidden meaning of his teachings: "To you has been given the secret of the kingdom of God, but for those outside everything is in parables" (Mark 4:11).

Scriptures are written with the understanding that what is appropriate for feeding to infants will no longer satisfy mature persons. The corollary is also true that no sensible mother would even try to feed her babe with the same whole food she gives her husband. So, too, in spiritual growth, what is given to spiritual babes is carefully prepared to nourish them in infancy, and when they mature they will receive food of another kind. "Everyone who lives on milk is unskilled in the word of righteousness, for he is a child. But solid food is for the mature, for those who have their faculties trained by practice" (Heb. 4:13-14).

In the early church those who studied the scriptures knew that the writings contained various strata of meaning. Today this approach is largely neglected. Each sect reads to find textual support for its own doctrinal statements, and dogma has supplanted the scriptures as the basis of teaching. Even theologians and biblical scholars, while engaged in the "search for the historical Jesus," have overlooked the central concern of the scriptures, which is to reveal the "universal Christ."

Jesus always pointed to the deeper meanings of his words by saying, "He who has ears to hear, let him hear," which is to say that a purified mind will comprehend the true significance of his teachings. At the same time, he warned his disciples not to cast their pearls before swine, not to spend truth foolishly on those who are unwilling to heed it, nor to reveal esoteric wisdom to those who are morally and intellectually unprepared to receive it.

The power generated by truth is turned to destructive ends in the hands of those whose motivations flow from selfish desires. But to those of purified heart and mind, truth was given to draw them more fully into the consciousness of the divine plan. Paul wrote:

> We impart a secret and hidden wisdom of God, which God decreed before the ages for our glorification. . . . As it is written, 'What no eye has seen, nor ear heard, nor the heart of man conceived, what God has prepared for those who love him,' God has revealed to us through the Spirit. For the Spirit searches everything, even the depths of God. For what person knows a man's thoughts except the Spirit of the man which is in him? So also no one comprehends the thoughts of God except the Spirit of God. Now we have received not the spirit of the world, but the Spirit which is from God, that we might understand the gifts bestowed on us by God. (1 Cor. 2:7-12)

The highest spiritual knowledge reflected in the Bible is not the result of sense perceptions, as is much of our normal knowledge of the world. Nor, says Paul, is deep spiritual awareness the result of thinking with the mind, as are many of the ideas we produce each day. Instead, spiritual truth is revealed to those who become aware, through meditation, of the presence of God's spirit within us. It is in this state that all is known, "even the depths of God." In this way Paul teaches that through meditation alone (the state that is beyond sense perception and thinking) does one experience the reality of eternal truth and absolute being through the awareness of God's spirit within the inner chamber of the self.

Origen, the great Christian scholar of the third century, applied to the Bible a three-level method of interpretation commonly used by the sages of ancient Eastern thought. According to this, scriptures have a "body," which is the external, factual, historical content that has been recorded. Above that foundation, scriptures have a "soul," which is the ethical meaning of the event as it is applied to the character or experience of their students. And, highest of all, there is the "spirit" of the scriptures, or the esoteric, allegorical meaning known only to those who have "the mind of Christ." To these qualified persons has been revealed (while they were in a state of superconscious meditation) the essential unity of the individual with God, the ultimate experience of human life toward which the scriptures are intended to lead us (*Origen, De Principis,* Preface, Book IV).

The Bible presents meditation as the technique by which persons may enter into full awareness of the "spirit" of the scriptures, into the experience of truth and essential being. Jesus, whose annointing as Christ signaled his own self-realization, declared: "I am the way, the truth and the life; no one comes to the Father but by me" (John 14:6). Christ-consciousness, achieved through meditation by sincere aspirants, then, is the direct experience of God as truth and truth as God. It is the way which reveals that the seeker, the path, and the goal are ultimately one. To come to the Father by way of Christ-consciousness is the only way in which one can attain to the state of union. The freedom that comes with the knowledge of the truth (John 8:32) is the experience expressed in the Master's words, "I and my Father are one" (John 10:30).

Meditation can be practiced by any sincere and disciplined disciple: "Let him who is thirsty come, let him who desires take the waters of life without price" (Rev. 22:17). Those who hunger and thirst after righteousness are promised satisfaction (Matt. 5:6).

The prophet Isaiah spoke of the meditative path as the way of holiness. In the passage that follows, the holy way is meditation, but it is clearly stated that it is a way open only to those of purified heart. (Jesus later was to say that only the pure of heart would see God.) The passage also describes the result of meditation: freedom from fear and its consequent destruction, deliverance from the threat of danger that springs from the sense of separateness and alienation in the external world, the realization of unity with God, and the experience of everlasting joy, bliss, and peace.

> And a highway shall be there,
> And it shall be called the Holy Way;
> the unclean shall not pass over it,
> And fools shall not err therein.
> No lion shall be there,
> Nor shall any ravenous beast come up on it;
> They shall not be found there,
> But the redeemed shall walk there.
> And the ransomed of the Lord shall return,
> And come to Zion with singing,
> With everlasting joy upon their heads;
> They shall obtain joy and gladness,
> And sorrow and sighing shall flee away.
>
> (Isaiah 35:8-10)

Here, Zion is a symbol for the state of exalted consciousness attained through meditation.

In the book of Psalms there are repeated references to meditation; the word *meditation*, in fact, appears here more often than in any other book of the Bible, and one of the most beautiful songs about meditation is Psalm 91. It begins with the verse:

> He who dwells in the shelter of the Most High,
> Who abides in the shadow of the Almighty,
> Will say to the Lord, "My refuge and my fortress;
> My God, in whom I trust."

Speaking thus of the meditative state as the "shadow of the Almighty," the psalmist goes on to describe the security, tranquility, joy, and attainment of the one who meditates. The Almighty One blesses the individual who approaches Him through meditation with the promise of deliverance, saying, "I will . . . show him My salvation."

The way of meditation is the path to which seekers for God are ultimately drawn. In Psalm 1 the righteous person is described as one who meditates on God's law by day and by night, asserting that his roots are securely planted beside the stream of life. "In all that he does, he prospers" (Ps. 1:6) for he is one with the fountainhead of prosperity.

Throughout the Bible there are numerous traditional symbols that represent the state of meditation and that give further insight into the depth of God-consciousness experienced by the sages of the Judeo-Christian heritage. For instance, one of the repeated symbols for meditation is silence. This state is praised in many of the Psalms, for it is only when one enters the silence beyond senses and thinking that one is directly aware of the presence of the Lord within: "Be still, and know that I am God" (Ps. 46:10). The seeker of eternal wisdom enters the meditative state for one purpose only—to be merged into the universal consciousness of the absolute: "For God alone my soul waits in silence" (Ps. 62:1).

Job, the sage afflicted by every sort of trial, clearly depicts the battle that every aspirant must wage against the domination of the senses and desires and the tyranny of mind. Finally stripped of every material, emotional, and mental attachment, Job is ready to heed the voice of the silence that leads to enlightenment: "Be silent, and I will teach you wisdom" (Job 33:33).

In the book of Revelation, an esoteric Christian guide to meditation, we find a reference to the passage of time while in a superconscious state: ". . . there was silence in heaven for about half an hour" (Rev. 8:1). Here the reference to "heaven" is also a symbol for meditation leading to superconscious awareness. And Jesus, in one of his clearest statements about meditation, directed his disciples to cultivate the habit of seeking regularly the silent inner chamber: "When you pray, go into your room and shut the door and pray to your Father who is in secret" (Matt. 6:6).

Another favorite biblical symbol of the state of superconscious meditation is "light," and Jesus spoke of Christ-consciousness as the light of perfect discrimination by which persons will know the real from the unreal: "I am the light of the world; he who follows me will not walk in darkness, but will have the light of life" (John 8:12). Light is also one of the most extensive symbols for ancient wisdom, having cosmic significance as well as being a symbol for spiritual enlightenment. It encompasses the creative power embodied in the self-manifestation of the absolute as well as the ultimate achievement of human life. The cosmic dimension of spiritual unfoldment is indicated in Paul's statement, "It is the God who said, 'Let light shine out of darkness,' who has shone in our hearts to give the light of the knowledge of the glory of God in the face of Christ" (2 Cor. 4:6).

As giver of light in the universe, the sun symbolizes the highest state of superconscious meditation. Once attained, the enlightened state does not disappear, for the consciousness of the individual remains focused "there" even in the midst of activity "here." The rising of the sun of enlightenment signifies the soul's final liberation from the bonds of the world: "Your sun shall no more go down, nor your moon withdraw itself; for the Lord will be your everlasting light, and your days of mourning shall be ended" (Is. 60:20).

Still another favorite biblical symbol for meditation is seen in the many references to the "temple." Throughout the whole Judeo-Christian tradition the temple is that place to which man goes to worship the Lord who dwells in the innermost chamber, the "Holy of Holies." The real significance of the temple, however, is not the physical building, or place of worship, but the temple within each person. "The God who made the world and everything in it, being Lord of heaven and earth, does not live in shrines made by man, nor is he served by human hands, as though he needed anything, since he himself gives to all men life and breath and everything. . . . He is not far from each one of us, for 'In him we live and move and have our being' " (Acts 17:24-28).

God is spirit and must be worshipped in the temple of spirit, in meditative union with Him. It is this innermost temple to which the prophet made reference when he said, "The Lord is in his holy temple: let all the earth keep silence before him (Hab. 2:20). Paul also wrote of this inner presence of God: "Do you not know that you are God's temple and that God's Spirit dwells in you? . . . For God's temple is holy, and that temple you are" (1 Cor. 3:16-17). Meditation begins when a person ceases looking for ultimate reality in that which is external to himself and becomes aware of the presence of God within. To go beyond oneself in search of God means to turn inward to the core of life, which is the essence of God's own being.

The greatest biblical insight related to the symbol of God's temple is found in the story of the boy Jesus' visit to the temple with his parents. As told in Luke 2:41-51, Jesus accompanies his parents to Jerusalem for the feast of the Passover. When his parents return home, Jesus remains in the temple. After three days they find him sitting in the temple among the teachers, and in response to their anxiety about his failure to return home with them, Jesus answers, "How is it that you sought me? Did you not know that I must be in my Father's house?"

Here the temple symbolizes the meditative state in which man experiences his essential unity with God. It is to this temple that we make our way again and again in search of joy, peace, wisdom, and real prosperity of spirit. The return of Mary and Joseph to their home represents our turning to the cares and life of the world (where renewed confusion is the inevitable result). With the attainment of self-realization, however, the consciousness of Christ remains focused in the temple, the Father's house. And even when attention is partially redirected to the world (Jesus did go home again with his parents), from that time on the individual consciousness remains essentially united with the universal consciousness of Christ. We learn through this story that enlightenment requires a universalization of consciousness, that the "sanctuary frame of mind" must be entered into and maintained throughout the whole day.

Additional symbols for the meditative state abound in the

Bible. A few more should be mentioned briefly before passing on to a consideration of the necessity for meditation in the life of the aspirant. The.state of meditation is sometimes symbolized by a dream, a vision, or a voice speaking as from God. The great prophet Elijah failed to discern God in external phenomena, but became aware of the divine presence as "a still small voice" within (1 Kings 19:12). Isaiah wrote of a similar experience: "Your ears shall hear a word behind you, saying, 'This is the way, walk in it" (Isaiah 30:21).

Mountains and other high places represent the lifting of consciousness above the mundane levels of sense and thinking. Throughout the whole chronicle of salvation history in the Old and New Testaments, the great events took place on a mountain or hill: Moses received the Ten Commandments in an exalted state of consciousness (on a hill); Jesus' Sermon on the Mount epitomizes New Testament spiritual awareness; the spiritual Transfirguration of Christ was set on a mountain. The word of the Lord comes time and again to his devout ones: "Go forth, and stand upon the mount before the Lord" (1 Kings 19:11). If God is to be perceived, if man is to unfold in universal consciousness, his awareness must be lifted above the "here" of sense and thought to the "there" of meditative union with the Father.

The sounding of the trumpet is another symbol for meditation and the state of superconsciousness. Jeremiah admonished his people: "Give heed to the sound of the trumpet" (Jer. 6:17). The trumpet call is one of the keys to the transition from one stage of meditation to another in the book of Revelation of John.

The head (sometimes depicted in art with a halo), altars, the ark of the covenant, anointment with oil, wellsprings, and many more symbols are additional means for conveying the deep allegorical truths about the meditative path to holiness.

Not only does the Bible contain such extensive symbolic reference to meditation as has been briefly surveyed, the Bible also offers to the serious student a deeper understanding of the importance—the necessity—of meditating.

As Jesus began his public teachings he announced the nature

of his mission: liberation. From the book of the prophet Isaiah we read:

> The Spirit of the Lord is upon me,
> Because he has anointed me to preach good news to the poor,
> He has sent me to proclaim release to the captives
> And recovery of sight to the blind,
> To set at liberty those who are oppressed,
> To proclaim the acceptable year of the Lord.

Then Jesus said, "Today this scripture has been fulfilled in your hearing" (Luke 4:18-21).

Jesus taught what he experienced himself: that liberation from the bonds of suffering and death comes only with the attainment of the state of Christ-consciousness. What was possible for the master, Jesus, is possible to those who follow his way: ". . .where I am you may be also" (John 14:3).

Jesus emphasized the contrast between bondage and eternal freedom by using images of death and life. He said, "I came that they might have life" (John 10:10), meaning that through meditation one may achieve liberation from that which binds him back to the level of life (which is characterized by suffering and death). The paradox of "living though dying" exemplifies the truth of awakening to eternal unity with God through the consciousness of the indwelling Christ: "I am the resurrection and the life; he who believes in me, though he die, yet shall he live, and whosoever lives and believes in me shall never die" (John 11:25-26).

With the awakening of the individual to the reality of a spiritual realm of eternal dimensions, all of one's experience begins to fall into proper perspective. What once seemed important is no longer attractive, for it is seen to be temporal and unsatisfying. There is a growing realization that before one can be a possessor of the eternal fruits of the spirit, he must rid himself of the attachments that bind him to earth. The *karmic* ties of desire that manifest in the passions must be overcome by redirecting all of our urges toward the one goal of liberation into unity with God. As

Jesus said to his followers: "Where your treasure is, there shall your heart be also" (Luke 12:34).

If a person's heart is attached to the objects, seen and unseen, of the physical and mental planes, he is locked into the cycle of temporality. When, however, his vision is lifted to the plane of spirit, he is freed for eternity. "The things which are seen are temporal," wrote Paul, "but the things which are not seen are eternal" (2 Cor. 4:13). Meditation is a necessary part of the aspirant's discipline because it is the only means available by which he can be freed from the lower attachments and begin to focus in the spiritual realm.

This shift in attention from the plane of sense perceptions to the realm of the spirit is identified in the Bible as the humanizing event, the "coming of age" of man through the realization of his human potential. In the Old Testament there are numerous references similar to this one from Ezekiel: "A new heart I will give you, and a new spirit I will put within you; and I will take out of your flesh the heart of stone and give you a heart of flesh. And I will put my spirit within you . . . . " (Ezek. 36:26-27). Henceforward, those who have received this spirit may attain the stature of full human dignity, which is the measure of the fulness of Christ (Eph. 4:13).

In the Bible the crowning achievement of man is to attain to the level of Christ-consciousness. This is the significance of the invitation of Jesus, "Follow me." This attainment of Christ-consciousness is portrayed in a verse from the last book of the Bible: "Then I looked, and lo, a white cloud, and seated on the cloud one like the son of man, with a golden crown on his head, and a sharp sickle in his hand" (Rev. 14:14). In this image the cloud represents the state of meditation, and the son of man is universalized- or Christ-consciousness attained through meditation. The golden crown directs our attention to the implicit claim that this state is the loftiest achievement of human life. And finally, the sickle is the faculty of discrimination sharpened by meditation, without which the spiritual harvest could not be reaped. Discrimination of the real from the unreal, the light from darkness and immortality from mortality, is that which leads to liberation from the bonds of temporality.

Christ-consciousness is not reached without constant effort on the part of the seeker, nor is the path of spiritual unfoldment an easy one to walk. Matthew records these words of Jesus: "Enter by the narrow gate; for the gate is wide and the way is easy, that leads to destruction, and those who enter by it are many. For the gate is narrow and the way is hard, that leads to life, and those who find it are few" (Matt. 7:13-14). As an explicit statement that to achieve deep meditation requires firm spiritual discipline and as an observation that many will fail to bring themselves to this level of realization, these words of Jesus parallel the words of Krishna in the Bhagavad Gita: "Out of many thousands among men, one may endeavor for perfection, and of those who have attained perfection, hardly one knows me in truth" (chapter 7, verse 3).

Difficult though it may be from the relative perspective of man, spiritual attainment is the culminating experience toward which all human life is striving. When men have finally exhausted their many desires for pleasures and powers, they become aware of the inner call to realize that which is eternal within themselves. When man is ready, he finds God waiting to reveal Himself both as the goal and as the path. "Behold, I stand at the door and knock; if any one hears my voice and opens the door, I will come into him and eat with him and he with me" (Rev. 3:20).

Jesus emphasized in his teaching that though the way appears difficult, to him who surrenders himself to the Lord the path of spiritual seeking is like looking for the path that leads home (the parable of the Prodigal Son). He taught that for those who are ready, the way will become clear. Progress becomes natural and even easy for those who are fully committed to the goal: "Come to me, all who labor and are heavy laden, and I will give you rest. Take my yoke upon you, and learn from me; for I am gentle and lowly in heart, and you will find rest for your souls. For my yoke is easy, and my burden is light" (Matt. 11:28-30). The word *yoke* is from the same Sanskrit root as the word *yoga;* both signify union, or binding together, and are used in appropriate contexts to indicate the preliminary disciplines as well as the achieved state of God-realization, or universal Christ-consciousness, which is the goal of all spiritual effort.

It is this striving, represented by the discipline of the yoke, that brings the seeker to the eventual realization of God. "I and the Father are One" (John 10:30), said the Christ. To enter into this consciousness is to become merged with God in a conscious way, for ". . .where I am you may be also" (John 14:3).

The Christ declared his continuous presence among his disciples: "Lo, I am with you always, to the close of the age" (Matt. 28:20). By this he meant that Self-realization (the realization of God within) is an ever-present possibility because it is an ever-present reality, though in a latent state of awareness. The power, awakened in the aspirant, to achieve this level of superconscious awareness, is the power of the indwelling Christ in every person. Jesus used the parable of the vine and branches to teach his followers that they have life only in God, not through any power of their own. We live in God; God lives in us. Our spiritual power is the power of God manifesting in us.

When we become aware of our true nature we realize that "apart from me you can do nothing" (John 15:5). At the same time the realization, through meditation, of our true nature shows us the unimagined heights we can attain. Jesus quoted the scriptures, saying, "you are gods," as evidence for the claim that "the Father is in me and I am in the Father" (John 10:34, 38). Knowing this, we are guided into the great truth, "the Spirit of truth whom the world cannot recieve" (John 14:17), the truth of which Christ said, "You shall know the truth, and the truth shall make you free" (John 8:32). The great truth of life is our essential and eternal unity with God, which truth, when it is experienced, frees us from all bondage of suffering and ignorance. Knowing this, a man knows all he needs to know, for he has become one with the eternal: "I, when I am lifted up from the earth, will draw all men to myself" (John 12:32).

To realize Christ in oneself, then, is the goal of the Christian's spiritual discipline. Symbolically, the seeker must die to the self of his lower nature and be born again in the higher consciousness of Christ within. Through meditation he becomes focused in the new dimension: "I have been crucified with Christ; it is no longer I who live, but Christ who lives in me" (Gal. 2:20).

Crucifixion and resurrection are a part of the Christian way to the realization of God. The old self of the lower nature is put to death; the new self of Christ-consciousness is raised to eternal life. Awareness of body, senses, emotions, and thoughts are withdrawn into the cave of death; the candle of realization shines brightly in the inner chamber of the self. The individual self dies; Christ lives within. By following this path of crucifixion and resurrection through meditation, the individual attains the goal: "Whatever gain I had, I counted as loss for the sake of Christ. Indeed I count everything as loss because of the surpassing worth of knowing Christ . . . that I may know him and the power of his resurrection" (Phil. 3:7-10).

In the book of the Revelation of John, this attainment is called the "crown of life" (Rev. 2:10), symbolizing achievement of the highest goal in life and the price of eternity through union with God. Jesus taught the surpassing value of Self-realization through inner awareness of the Father and told his disciples that they could expect to know only prolonged death and suffering so long as they sought to save their lives through attachment to physical and mental securities. "For whoever would save his life will lose it, and whoever loses his life for my sake will find it. For what will it profit a man if he gains the whole world and forfeits his life?" (Matt. 16:25).

To reach the end for which meditation is the means is to experience the bliss, wisdom, and peace of God. Jesus spoke of this peace as his great gift to his followers: "Peace I leave with you; my peace I give to you" (John 14:27). In the peace of God is the steadiness of knowing that there will never be separation from the Father. This great affirmation of life is summarized by Paul in his letter to the Romans: "For I am sure that neither death, nor life, nor angels, nor principalities, nor things present, nor things to come, nor powers, nor height, nor depth, nor anything in all creation, will be able to separate us from the love of God in Christ Jesus our Lord" (Rom. 8:38-39).

The story of Stephen provides an appropriate conclusion to this account of the place of meditation in the Bible. As told in the Acts of the Apostles, his story is a revelation of that glorious experience that comes to a God-enlightened man who knows that nothing can destroy his essential union with God. He is described as a man "full of the Spirit and of wisdom" (6:3) whose face "was like the face of an angel" (6:15) in the hour of his realization. The culmination of his unfoldment into full awareness of God came in the form of a vision: "He, full of the Holy Spirit, gazed into heaven and saw the glory of God, and Jesus standing at the right hand of God; and he said, Behold I see the heavens opened, and the Son of man standing at the right hand of God" (Acts 7:55-56).

The Bible is filled with these and many more references to meditation and the attainment of God-realization. There is no other goal worthy of our commitment, and, as we have seen, the Christ of the Bible is both the power and the symbol of that high attainment to which we are called.

The Development of Christian Meditation in Light of Yoga

Justin O'Brien, D.Th.

Among modern Christians there is a renewed interest in the meaning and direction of their spiritual life. At the forefront of this concern is the growing attraction for the practice of meditation and contemplation. Some believers, however, view these practices as highly novel—even offensive—and consider them an inroad by Eastern non-Christian influences or, at best, a temporary fad.

Surprising as it may seem to them, there is ample precedence for meditation and contemplation rooted in the Bible and eagerly developed from the inception of Christianity. This rich tradition espoused techniques and exercises that centered around achieving both inner quiet and the expansion of consciousness.

For centuries, then, the terms meditation, contemplation, and prayer have been variously commented upon in the writings of their practitioners. The range of interpretations accruing to these terms has often led to problems regarding their meaning and practical applicability. A clarification is needed.

A general survey of the inauguration of these terms within the growth of organized Christianity will trace some of the strands of meaning that became entangled and that produced the eventual confusion prevailing today. At the same time, the meaning of these terms as portrayed in representative textbooks on spirituality will be examined in comparison to the ancient yoga tradition.

The Double Tradition of Christian Spirituality

The event of Jesus Christ inspired in his followers a desire to pursue a life of ultimate significance. Amidst the Jewish and Roman cultures of the first three centuries, Christians gradually organized themselves into various groups of churches and adapted their master's teachings to their surroundings. These "followers of the way," as they were called, sought to engender in themselves the scriptural admonition, "You, therefore, are to be perfect, even as your heavenly father is perfect" (Matt. 5:48). Paul, the thirteenth apostle, mentions that Christians are "called to be saints" (Rom. 1:7, 8:28; 1 Cor. 1:2), since "this is the will of God, your sanctification" (1 Thess. 4:3). While the exact adaptation of the Christian way of life was left to the individual churches, their overall direction was quite clear: Christians were to lead a life of evangelical integrity; that is, a life of poverty or detachment from worldly goods, chasteness, and obedience to the will of God.

The first two centuries of Christianity showed a twofold development in spirituality: institutional and monastic. After Pentecost the first bishops and priests were concerned primarily with the moral standards of their communities. These leaders wrote many letters that convey the direction, problems, and pressures of the time. The Epistle to Diognetus in the second century mentions that

> Christians do not differ from other men in country or language or peculiarity of life. . . . For there are no towns set apart for them, nor language spoken by them alone, and there is no eccentricity in their manner of living. . . . They inhabit the towns of the Greeks or the barbarians, as their lot may be, and while following the customs of the country in which they are, whether in the matter of clothing or food or other habits, they lead an admirable sort of life which in the eyes of all men is taken to be a prodigy. Each one of them dwells in his country, but as a stranger; they share in everything as citizens and endure everything as if they did not belong to the country. . . they are in the flesh, but they live not after the flesh. They obey the law but by their manner of life they are above the law.[1]

In their newfound approach to life, most Christians continued to live as ordinary citizens while maintaining a definite moral outlook on culture that was inoffensive (although somewhat baffling) to their Roman neighbors. For the next two centuries the Roman authorities became increasingly intolerant of the Christians and finally branded them atheists and enemies of the state. The terrible persecutions in the name of the Roman religion reached such atrocities, including martyrdom for hundreds of believers, that many Christians feared for their lives and abandoned their commitment to Christ rather than endure torture and martyrdom. The trials and oppressions finally ceased, so that the catacomb Christians could then practice their way unopposed, as a result of Constantine, the new Christian emperor, declaring Christianity to be the state religion in A.D. 313.

Ironically, in moving toward the future, the Christian hierarchy organized its communities by modeling them upon Roman law and politics. The biblical message was then interpreted within this institutional framework.

Along with this institutional approach to spirituality, there existed another rarer phenomenon: the monastic ascetics. The Greek word *monos* meaning "alone" is the root of the words "monk" and "monastery." These terms originally meant a person or place where one lived solitarily. Men and women responded to the challenge of living up to the scriptural injunctions with a fervor and intensity that awed most believers. From such ascetics' own writings and from eyewitness accounts of this period come descriptions of their austere daily regimes centered around prayer and meditation:

> And when he [Anthony] had made an end of these things, he forthwith became a solitary monk, and he took no care for anything whatsoever except his soul, and he began to train himself in the habits of the strictest abstinence and self-denial. And he took up his abode there in the desert by himself and he shut himself in and he laid in a supply of bread once every six months. . . . He dwelt there in a place which was like a cleft in the rocks, with the intention of seeing no man and of being seen by none and he had his abode there for very many years.[2]

Some of the monks lived on dry bread; some ate only once a week. Some wore untanned skins of animals; some went naked. Most monks slept little and lived in caves or outdoors without shelter. Their poverty was absolute, and endurance was their most cultivated virtue. The following advice of a monk to a beginner was not too exaggerated from that typically found: "Eat grass, wear grass, and sleep on grass, and then thy heart will become like iron."[3]

Most of the ascetics pursued a career that was incompatible with worldly values; their concern was for the inner life of the spirit. The decadence of Roman society included too many distractions that could impede their commitment. The dangers of living during the Roman persecutions mentioned above, as well as their profound desire for Christian perfection, no doubt influenced their self-exile to the wilderness. The flight to the desert resulted in a diversity of life-styles. Those who chose to live alone were called anchorites or hermits, while those choosing companionship in small groups were known as cenobites, meaning "life in common."

The trek to the wilderness later captured the imaginations of Christians on a fairly large scale. There were thousands of representatives in Egypt, Palestine, Syria, and Asia Minor by the end of the fourth century.

> And there were living in that mountain about seven thousand brethren, and in the monastery in which the blessed Pachomius himself lived there were living one thousand three hundred brethren; and besides these there were also other monasteries, each containing about three hundred, or two hundred, or one hundred monks, who lived together; and they all toiled with their hands and lived thereby, and with whatsoever they possessed which was superfluous for them they provided or fed the nunneries which were there.[4]

The three names most associated with the inauguration of desert life are Paul of Thebes, Anthony of Thebaid, and Pachomius.[5] It was Pachomius who later composed the first rule for cenobites to live in small communities. This was in approximately A.D. 320. Since the communities were more concerned about ritual and group prayer as well as the common life, they were less austere than their hermit neighbors.

> Each day those whose week of service it was rose up and attended to their work; and others attended to the cooking, and others set out the tables and laid upon them bread and cheese, and vessels of vinegar and water. And there were some monks who went in to partake of food at the third hour of the day, and others at the sixth hour, and others at the ninth hour, and others in the evening, and others who ate once a day only; and there were some who ate only once a week; and according as each one of them knew the letter which had been laid upon him, so was his work. Some worked in the paradise (i.e., the orchard), and some in the gardens, and some in the blacksmith's shop, and some in the baker's shop, and some in the carpenter's shop, and some in the fuller's shop, and some wove baskets and mats of palm leaves, and one was a maker of nets, and one was a maker of sandals, and one was a scribe; now all these men as they were performing their work were repeating the Psalms and the Scriptures in order. And there were there large numbers of women who were nuns, and who closely followed this rule of life also.[6]

Origins of Meditation in Christianity

In their daily practices the Christian ascetics borrowed both techniques and attitudes from contemporary non-Christian sources. One can trace instances of Roman stoicism (Epictetus and Cicero) as well as Platonic and Neoplatonic theory in their conceptions of the spiritual life. Similarly, the Christian theologians borrowed from the philosophical categories of Hellenic and Roman thought in explaining the theology of Christianity. One can easily read, for example, in St. Augustine, the evidence of his use of Plato's dialogues. Even as late as the thirteenth century, Thomas Aquinas likewise espoused Aristotelian concepts within theological contexts. Thus it is not surprising that a careful examination of the philosophy of human nature implied by most of the desert monks in their writings shows a definite tendency for Neoplatonic interpretation.

Since many of the monks were uneducated, their attempts to advance in the spiritual life also came by way of experimentation. Consequently, ascetic excesses are notable in the accounts of their lives. It is from these same individuals, however, that the practice of meditation evolved. This is not to say that Christ and the apostles or the ordinary believer did not meditate. There is sufficient scriptural evidence to the contrary. The Nag Hammadi scriptures seem to indicate that some Gnostic communities included meditation as an essential practice for Christian growth. Also, the Jewish Essene communities who practiced meditation were well known to Jesus and his disciples. Institutional Christianity, however, did not emphasize the role of meditation. The ascetics and monks are the most notable examples of Christians who seriously involved themselves with meditation.

Since their lives were committed to the imitation of Christ's, every one of their human acts, internal as well as external, was associated in their minds with this religious quest. One could say that everything they did was justified or approached from a religious perspective. Their entire day was interpreted as a series of prayerful actions motivated by the intention of bringing themselves interiorly closer to the mind and heart of Jesus Christ. Within this perspective, meditation was practiced as a form of prayer—attunement with God. It was an indispensable pious exercise of the ascetics' daily life. Their commingling of prayer and meditation would not be unexpected, since their activities were always viewed from a religious standpoint. Even their breathing practices and bodily postures were put within a category of prayer. Thus, the valuable techniques and results of meditation, although capable of being effectively engaged in without a religious context, were nevertheless given a religious slant and put at the service of the goal of prayer.

From the anchorite Evagrius of Pontus (A.D. 345-399), Christians received the first codified treatise on monastic prayer. Some of Evagrius' assertions on prayer show the juxtaposition of prayer and meditation. He mentions the traditional description that "prayer is an ascent of the intellect to God."[7] For Evagrius the notion of intellect (Greek, *nous*) had nothing to do with the rational mind. In his understanding of human consciousness, he divides it into two major levels. The rational or discursive level of consciousness depends upon the bodily senses to provide the data for thought. Exercising this part of consciousness did not lead one into the true realm of prayer. One had to supersede this level and arrive at the higher level that Evagrius called intellection. Reasoning, the customary operation of the mind during everyday activities, is one level, while the higher level, intellection, dispenses with ideas and sense impressions and is an immediate intuitive awareness. Because of this division of consciousness, he further mentions that "you cannot attain pure prayer while entangled in material things and agitated by constant cares. For prayer means the rejection of concepts."[8] Again he states that "prayer is the energy which accords with the dignity of the intellect; it is the intellect's true and highest activity."[9] And again, "Blessed is the intellect that is completely free from forms during prayer . . .and has acquired complete freedom from sensations during prayer."[10] For Evagrius, the intellect is divine and thus is capable of achieving a profound stillness (*hesychia*). The deepest realm of intellect places one into divine awareness—the very goal of the Christian way. Evagrius considered this the supreme mystical state, the deification of man that the monks speak of as the Christian's rightful destiny.

The yoga tradition of meditation coincides with this inner dynamism as described by Evagrius. Patanjali, the codifier of yoga (200 B.C.), similarly indicates that when one is no longer bothered by sense impressions nor distracted by ideas or concepts, but has brought feelings, thoughts, and remembrances under control, then one becomes aware of his full identity. In yoga the primary practice that achieves this inner stilling of the mind is meditation. Both Evagrius and Patanjali recognize that the pursuit of ultimate significance, whether placed within a religious context or not, employs the same quieting of the mind's operations.

For Evagrius, when one lives out of this inner communion, one's entire life is then sacramental; that is, any act is a sacred performance, motivated from this highest state of divine awareness. In the ancient yogic text, the Bhagavad Gita, Krishna similarly tells his student, Arjuna, that when actions are performed from an attitude of divine service, they become acts of worship.

In carefully assessing the inner dynamics of these two traditions, a virtual identity emerges. The depiction of the process of stillness differs only because of the pious symbols and historical context within which it is expressed.

The Jesus Prayer

As the centuries passed, variations of prayer and meditation enriched monastic spirituality. The most notable emphasis came in the acceptance of the interior process called the Jesus Prayer. As early as the fourth century, Abbot Makarios of Egypt answered an aspirant's question about how to pray by telling him to say, "Lord, save me."[11] It is quite likely that the Jesus Prayer developed from the *Kyrie eleison* "Lord have mercy" found constantly in the Christian liturgy. Although other monks used abbreviations of the prayer such as "Jesus have mercy" or "Christ have mercy," the precise formula of the Jesus Prayer—"Lord Jesus Christ, son of God, have mercy upon me"—achieved its final form during the sixth century when an Egyptian hermit, Abba Philemon, explicitly used it in this manner.[12]

The repetition of the Jesus Prayer was generally combined with the respiratory process as well as with concentration on the region of the heart. An experienced monk would instruct the aspirant in the exact coordination of breath and interior utterance. As John Climacus (A.D. 580-650) remarks in his famous treatise on spirituality, *The Ladder of Paradise,* "May the name of Jesus be united with your breath; then you will understand the value of solitude (*hesychia*)."[13] It was the Jesus Prayer tradition more than any other type of prayer that became identified with Hesychasm, the practice of stilling the mind. It is interesting to note that in the instructions of the monks Callistus and Ignatius, there is an emphasis upon coordinating the breath with the mind's attention that has also always been an indispensable step within the yoga tradition of meditation:

> At this point it seems to us suitable to expound a certain natural method of the blessed Nicephorus of entering the heart by attention through breathing, which contributes to the concentration of thoughts. After quoting the evidence of many holy fathers concerning inner life, this holy man says the following from his own experience: "You know, brother, how we breathe: we breathe the air in and out. On this is based the life of the body and on this depends its warmth. So, sitting down in your cell, collect your mind, lead it into the path of the breath along which the air enters in, constrain it to enter the heart together with the inhaled air, and keep it there. Keep it there, but do not leave it silent and idle; instead give it the following prayer: 'Lord Jesus Christ, Son of God, have mercy upon me.' Let this be its constant occupation, never to be abandoned. For this work, by keeping the mind free from dreaming, renders it unassailable to suggestions of the enemy and leads it to divine desire and love."[14]

The Consolidation of Monasticism

Differences in emphasis and development between Roman and Byzantine Christianity were evident in their approaches to spirituality and hence to meditation. Western Christianity attempted to develop the implications of the Gospels within a Roman organizational framework. Civil and religious spheres grew closer together during the Middle Ages in feudal Europe and religious practices became more regulated by legislation and Church authority. It is true that monasteries still retained their individual autonomy, but monastic observances were becoming increasingly standardized. It became mandatory for the monks to assemble for the solemn chanting of prayers and scripture called the Divine Office. This praying in common at set hours daily assumed the central act of the monastic life.

Meanwhile, the hermetic tradition survived in the West, although not to the vast extent that it did in the Middle East. This Western tradition, too, began to change after the large monasteries erected vaults beneath their ground floors for the local hermits. These rooms or cells adjoined one another, enabling their inhabitants to communicate discretely. Thus the cenobite life slowly eclipsed the desert ideal of strict isolation. Living within a monastery became the norm for those seeking the higher way. This legislative development was brought about by St. Benedict of Nursia (A.D. 480-547), the founder of Monte Cassino Abbey in Italy. His rule for regulating the monastic schedule became the prototype for the various monasteries that eventually became a federation in the tenth century. No doubt meditation, especially the hesychast form, was known to the monks, but its explicit endorsement is nowhere mentioned in Benedict's rule.

Byzantine Christianity was not as structured as the Roman Church, and its monks followed primarily the rules of St. Pachomius and St. Basil, which were less regimented. Anchorites presented a problem; many wandering hermits were considered an embarrassment to the monasteries and towns and were eventually accused of disturbing society. In response to these complaints, Emperor Justinian issued decrees in the sixth century that compelled eremitical monks to live in monasteries.

Still, there was an admiration for those monks who felt called to the solitary life. The problem was handled in a unique way. As a monk progressed in the monastic life, he could eventually arrive at sufficient maturity where he would decide to leave the cloister and retire to the desert. In this way he was still connected to the monastery but had sufficient liberty to satisfy his desire for a closer union with God in solitude. This development in Eastern monastic spirituality is described in the *Ladder of Paradise* by St. John Climacus, who was himself a hermit who had started out as a cenobite. Thus, the principal reason that the eremitical tradition never died out in the East was the profound conviction that it was the crowning path of spirituality.

The Regimentation of the Spiritual Life

A similar respect for the monastic vocation was preserved in the West. According to Pourrat in his history of Christian spirituality, "from the sixth century, and during the great part of the Middle Ages, spirituality in the West is found almost exclusively in the monastic rules, which were drawn up in great numbers."[15] Nevertheless, following a rule did not constrain the most flourishing experimental period in the history of Christian spirituality. For almost a thousand years, the approaches of saints and mystics to Christian sanctity were exceedingly diverse, as illustrated by the variety of monasteries, convents, and schools of spirituality that emerged in Europe.

The Middle Ages displayed a novel creativity as well as a reliance upon traditional texts in regard to the theoretical details of meditative states of consciousness. Many monasteries and schools of spirituality accepted as their principal guide the writings of Dionysius the Areopagite. Dionysius understood the spiritual journey primarily as a meditative process leading to a supra-rational knowledge of God in which one knows immediately and directly. This direct vision at first obscures the mind with a dazzling light, the intensity of which in turn causes a darkness to envelop reason and the senses. He understood this darkness as the presence of God. As one continued to meditate and enter more deeply into the silence of this darkness, one was led finally into the very light that initially produced the darkness.

In one of his principle works, called *De Mystica Theologia* (*The Hidden Knowledge of God*), he counsels:

> In the earnest exercise of mystical contemplation, you leave the senses and the operations of reason and all things that the senses or reason can perceive, to the end that you raise yourself by this unknowing to union with Him who is above all being and all knowledge; that is, to raise yourself by absolute detachment from yourself and all things, stripped of everything and free from every hindrance to that stream of divine brightness coming forth from this inner obscurity.[16]

The texts of Dionysius were attributed to Denis, traditionally held to be the bishop of Paris and the companion of St. Paul. Thus great reverential deference was paid to his words. Ironically, these texts were later proven to belong to the sixth century, most likely written by an anonymous monk in Syria. They were finally translated into Latin, entering the West officially in A.D. 877.

Many saints and theologians found the Dionysian texts a reputable map for their spiritual journey. The medieval theologians and monastic founders assimilated the Dionysian doctrine on meditation into their own writings. Scotus Erigena, the Victorines, Albertus Magnus, Bonaventure, Thomas Aquinas, Meister Eckhart, Henry Suso, and many other authors cite the Syrian texts as spiritual authority.

Echoes of Hesychasm are also found in many Western writings of this time. Richard of St. Victor (died 1173) describes the highest state of spirit as "the hidden place of inner quietness, the sanctuary of the highest tranquility."[17] Edmund Rich of Canterbury (1180-1240) speaks of first contemplating one's wondrous nature and God's beneficence. He tells the student, after being awed by the goodness and beauty of life itself, to "put every corporal image outside your heart, and let your naked intention fly up above all human reasoning."[18] The anchoress Lady Julian of Norwich (1343-1413) says, "The soul is united to God when she is truly pacified in herself."[19] St. Catherine of Siena (1347-1380) speaks of the peace achieved through meditation: "The state of the soul is then a feeling of such utter peace and tranquility that it seems to her that her heart and her bodily being and all both within and without is immersed in an ocean of utmost peace."[20] The anonymous fourteenth century English author of the well-known works *The Cloud of Unknowing* and *The Book of Privy Counseling* makes use of a phrase similar to the "naked intention" used earlier by Rich:

> By pursuing your meditation to the farthest reaches and ultimate frontiers of thought, you will find yourself in the end, on the essential ground of being with the naked perception and

blind awareness of your own being. . . . Leave the awareness of
your being unclothed of all thoughts about its attributes, and
your mind quite empty of all particular details. . . . This blind
awareness . . . will far surpass the value of any particular
thought, no matter how sublime.[21]

These works reiterate the Dionysian doctrine that carried its
influence even into the late Middle Ages with the writings of John
of the Cross and Teresa of Avila.

After the sixteenth century, the brilliant tapestry of medieval
spirituality shrank to a cloth of just a few colors. An exciting new
secular era broke upon the unprepared Christian West. The
mixture of the discovery of the New World, the Protestant
Reformation, the Galilean embarrassment, and the mounting
tensions between church and state produced such civil and
religious upheavals that the Christian leaders enforced a siege
mentality. The creative liberty enjoyed by men and women in
exploring the steps to their spiritual destiny became more and
more curtailed. Methods and exercises were closely scrutinized
and increasingly standardized. For the supposed protection of
Christians, a suppressive atmosphere was legislated throughout
Europe. Spiritual orthodoxy lost its flexibility and became
restricted to fixed methods that required official approval.

In an effort to defend itself against other, erroneous types of
spirituality, Catholics and Protestants set up carefully monitored
instructions on the unfoldment of the spiritual life along with its
limitations and dangers. The aspirants were obliged to follow
certain orthodox methods. Within this strict milieu, experimentation and unfamiliar methods, however valid, brought suspicion
and censure upon the innovators.

The sixteenth century also saw a general reformation by
Roman Christianity taking place during the forty-five year period
of the Council of Trent. From this point on, no new monastic
orders were permitted to be instituted. Adjusting to the signs of
these times, religious communities no longer were to be involved in
the eremitical life. The only exceptions made were for the monastic

orders already in existence. Instead, new congregations were formed for the purpose of active engagement in the needs and growth of society. One of the most outstanding of these was the Society of Jesus, also called the Jesuits, founded by St. Ignatius of Loyola.

The impact of Roman Christianity's attitude towards the secular era changed the emphasis in practices of meditation. Pourrat remarks that "in the days of St. Ignatius' conversion, meditation had become methodized, prayer regulated and the whole spiritual life organized and its various exercises so coordinated as to create a real system of moral reformation."[22] Up to this time, the goal of meditation was to achieve Christ-consciousness. Now the goal became one of moral conversion to the life of Jesus. To illustrate how this transformation was to take place, let us examine one of the most popular methods of meditation for these new religious communities—the Spiritual Exercises of St. Ignatius.

The exercises are divided into four weeks of meditations that are generally guided by a retreat director. The first week is designed to help the aspirant to purify his soul and put his life in order; the aim of the second week is to lead the soul to a greater knowledge of and love for Jesus Christ; the third week is devoted to freeing the will from the psychological obstacles that stand in the way of a decision to follow Christ; and the fourth week is intended to purify the heart in the highest degree from false attachments to creatures, goods, or worldly ambition and honor.

For those who are unable to follow the four-week regime, an intensive eight-day retreat condensing the entire method can be used. Whichever length is taken, there is no omission of the following four key meditation steps:

1. The aspirant begins with a preparatory prayer in which he begs that his intentions and actions be solely directed to the service and honor of the Divine Majesty.

2. He conjures in his imagination the composition of place. If the

object of meditation is a biblical scene, he stirs up the appropriate images relating to that scene in order to dwell upon it. Should the object of meditation be sin, for example, one may fantasize ugly scenes in order to provoke a horror for sin. After sufficient time, he petitions God for the special graces to be obtained by this meditative step.

3. The central portion of the meditation involves the exercise of the various faculties of the soul—the memory, the intellect, and the will. The memory vividly portrays the material or object to be discursively meditated upon. The intellect then reflects upon the object and discerns what practical applications to one's daily life may be drawn from this consideration. The will deliberately arouses feelings of devotion about these discursive truths or awakens a feeling of the presence of God. With the affections amplified, one's will should now decide on and carry out a practical resolution inspired by the aforesaid process.

4. One should conclude meditation with devout colloquies with the saints or the Godhead, and survey this entire meditative process noting its imperfections and how to improve it.

The entire period for this method may last twenty minutes or as long as an hour, depending upon one's fervor or available moments.[23]

The Ignatian method of meditation and other similar methods carefully regulated one's moral transformation. Instead of using the more spontaneous and creative writings of the Desert Fathers and the saints of the Middle Ages, manuals that divided and subdivided the stages of the interior life were written for aspirants. They gave a finality to the terms and meaning of spiritual progress. The practical impact of these writings left the impression that they were the only methods available by which to achieve perfection. Consequently, many of the older writings were neglected for the sake of producing a unified out- look on the constitution of official spirituality. This organized approach of approved instructions has come down into the twentieth century.

The Confusion of Terms

Despite such rigid interpretations of meditation, the monastic traditions found in both Eastern and Western Christianity retained a similar appreciation regarding the dynamics of meditation. Yet each group produced practitioners whose writings show an originality in their contributions to the inner life. The authors' writings obviously reflected both their own cultural images and their concerns for providing proper guidance, since they were aware that their texts would be utilized as instruction manuals for aspirants. While the theories of meditation, contemplation, and prayer were assigned to the same ambit of spiritual progress, the words used to describe one's experience of each were often interchanged. The need for precision in language did not seem to be an issue. In fact, the higher states of meditation are exceedingly difficult to describe in any graphic manner since the experience is devoid of images and concepts. The practitioners often resorted to poetic description or made use of symbols that only hinted at these transcendental moments. Use of a wide leeway in choice of terms was often the case.

After the Reformation, however, this poetic license was radically reduced to an orthodoxy in line with the defensive posture of the church authorities. The composition of spiritual writings now insured a standard vocabulary and a fixing of the terms. An unforeseen problem immediately occured in the official acceptance of a rather fluid association between prayer, meditation, and contemplation. In attempting to elucidate these experiences with distinct categories of meaning, theologians increased the confusion of terms by misdefining them.

In order to illustrate this misunderstanding, two representative spiritual manuals explaining meditation and contemplation have been selected from the many volumes written within the Christian tradition. One manual by Reverend A. Tanquerey entitled *The Spiritual Life* has been used extensively in monasteries and convents in America and Europe. It states:

> The terms meditation and mental prayer are often inter-
> changed. When differentiated, the former is applied to that
> form of mental prayer wherein considerations and reasonings
> predominate and which, owing to this, is called discursive
> meditation.[24]

A more contemporary manual, *The Theology of Christian
Perfection,* written by two monks, states that

> discursive meditation can be defined as a reasoned application
> of the mind to some supernatural truth in order to penetrate its
> meaning, love it and carry it into practice with the assistance of
> grace. The distinguishing note of meditation is that it is a
> reasoned or discursive type of prayer, and therefore attention is
> absolutely indispensable. As soon as one ceases to reason or
> discourse, he ceases to meditate. He may have given way to
> distraction, deliberately turned his mind to something else,
> passed on to affective prayer or contemplation, but without
> discursus there is no meditation.[25]

Both manuals consider meditation as an exercise of prayer;
indeed, a lower form of prayer suitable only for beginners on the
spiritual path. Whatever method of discursive meditation or
mental prayer one selected was viewed as only a temporary means
to spiritual progress. Beginners were cautioned that these meditational methods could get in the way of progress. The road to
perfection demanded that one eventually dispense with meditation.

The manuals portray contemplation as a more advanced
stage than meditation. Contemplation is seen as a supernatural
gift from God, rendered gratuitously to the aspirant. The aspirant
has no claim upon it, nor can he induce it by his own efforts. Like
meditation, it is also understood as a form of prayer:

> Contemplation is an operation in which one experiences the
> happy blending of the cognitive and the affective powers in an
> activity which is at once intuitive and delightful.[26]

> Contemplation is produced through the operation of the gifts of
> the Holy Spirit. . . . consequently one cannot contemplate
> mystically whenever he wishes.[27]

The manuals are careful to insist that since the object of contemplation is the Godhead, the human faculties by themselves are incapable of apprehending such a profound object. Some condescension on the part of God must be involved if mortals are to contemplate him. God, in his infinite mercy, must bestow or infuse upon the human faculties the added capacity to reach out, as it were, to an object that normally exceeds the mind's field of operation. In this way, the divine bestowal of grace makes the act of infused contemplation not a natural act of human cognition, but a supernatural act, an act that is above and beyond the normal range of human endeavor. Contemplation may be performed only on God's terms. The contemplative act of awareness remains irreproachably outside of man's finest capacities.

This is a strange paradox. The spiritual manuals were meant to guide aspirants to the highest states of sanctity. Yet their complexity of prolix terms and complicated distinctions make their efficacy as guides practically nil. The simple yet profound tools of meditation and contemplation that guided the saints were thus reduced to beginner's practices or unattainable gifts.

The Eclipse of the Mystical Life

During the modern period, the emphasis of spiritual direction by many theologians, priests, and ministers turned from emphasizing a contemplative spirituality to forging a good character in believers. The goal of institutional spirituality was to protect people from sin and prepare them for heaven. The goal of monastic living, which had long been to achieve stillness and union with God in meditation, became submerged to the above-mentioned goal of the institutional church.

The spiritual manuals, then, are seen through this rather pessimistic atmosphere. The spiritual quest was limited to acquiring Christian virtues, and as a result of this moral concern, one's use of prayer, meditation, and concentration was put almost exclusively at the service of cultivating a moral individual rather than expanding his consciousness. One cannot help but ask a persistent question: What has happened to the profound experiences and the high states of consciousness reported in the lives of the hermits and mystics?

The direction of the spiritual life as legislated by the Council of Trent had its effects both on monastic living and on the lives of ordinary Christians: standardized practices were decreed; monastic life became complicated (it was not the simple life of the ancient tradition any longer); and the methods of meditation of the ancients were practiced less and less while their place was filled with community activities. Added to the Divine Office were other duties such as daily liturgy and works of charity that supported the moral development of the virtues. The amount of time spent in meditation and contemplation was enormously reduced. This consequently produced a very different atmosphere in monastic living. The achievements of the Desert Fathers and the medieval mystics were seen to be such a distant goal that they were classified, even in spiritual texts, as a rare grace that most people could never practically hope to obtain.

Contemporary Meditation

Among all the events that have occurred in our disruptive century, there are two that have had very significant consequences upon the development of the practice of meditation. The first event occurred in 1962 when the largest church in Western Christianity, Roman Catholicism, underwent a revolution in self-examination. This event was called the Second Vatican Council. For three consecutive years in Rome, representatives from Catholic dioceses of the world met, discussed, and debated the Church's position vis-à-vis the modern world and its problems of meaningful survival. The Council took as its watchword *aggiornamento*—an updating, a deliberate admission that the Church was falling behind the times and needed drastic revisions in order to become relevant to contemporary society. For many of the professionally religious, these new changes came too late. In the aftereffect, thousands of religious men and women resigned from monasteries, convents, and religious houses to join the ranks of the laity.

The second event occurred shortly thereafter. Spiritual teachers from the Eastern hemisphere traveled to the West and exposed thousands of people to the Oriental traditions of meditation. Unknown to most Christians, these traditions showed a remarkable resemblance in methodology and content to the ancient Christian tradition of meditation.

A strange reversal resulted from this combination of events. As more and more Christians began to accept the experiential truth of these practices, the laity took the lead in incorporating meditation into their daily lives. The surprising result is that institutional monasteries have begun to follow suit. In some of these groups one can find a return to the early Christian meditative texts that were so prevalent during the first fifteen hundred years of Christianity's existence, and that had been ignored for so long.

Meditation in Yoga: A Comparison

For contemporary Christians, then, who may be interested in meditation, it is advantageous to compare the yoga tradition of meditation with the customary theological meanings of meditation and contemplation for the sake of avoiding misunderstandings in their renewed roles in the spiritual life. The term meditation possesses an entirely different meaning and use in yogic writings than in the Christian manuals. It is not employed in any religious context, nor does it presuppose any particular theological framework. Similar to the Christian manuals, it directs its techniques to a practical goal, but instead of concentrating on the moral growth of the individuals (which is only a part of the preparation for meditation), yoga meditation strives to transform the individual by expanding his awareness. This enlargement is not an increase nor a refinement of ideas or images but a systematic inner experiencing of richer levels of reality.

In his Yoga Sutras, Patanjali classifies the ancient experiential tradition of yoga meditation as both a superconscious state of being and as a process that leads to that state. He defines it as "the uninterrupted flow of the mind towards an inner object."[28] The goal of the meditator is to perdure in the state; one does not outgrow this accomplishment but deepens it increasingly.

In Patanjali's analysis of human consciousness, there is a distinction between this non-imaginative and non-conceptual state of consciousness and the expression of this same consciousness in its conjunction with the human body. Consciousness ordinarily utilizes the body as its instrument during the combined psychophysical acts of sensations, imaginations, and conceptualizations that mediate the customary knowledge of the external world. The physical body is the organic correlate to the mental operations of consciousness that are collectively referred to as the *antahkarana.* So far, the psychosomatic structure found in the Yoga Sutras would be amenable to the Christian manuals' outline of the body-mind complex. Yet, there is a major difference between the manuals and the Yoga Sutras. The manuals insist that the mind or consciousness in itself is inactive or passive, that it cannot perform cognition without the instrumentality of the mental faculties being stimulated by the input from the external world. By contrast, the Yoga Sutras assert that the soul's consciousness subsists in operation, that it never ceases to be in a state of perfect awareness. While the soul may utilize the antahkarana, or the mental faculties, in conjunction with the sense organs, there is, nevertheless, no essential dependence upon them. In fact, through the continual practice of yogic meditation, the practitioner gradually experiences a differentiation in awareness between the discursive contents of his mind and his immanent act of awareness. This is comparable to Evagrius' view of the totality of human consciousness mentioned earlier.

In the modern Christian methods of meditation, one remains within the field of his mental faculties and dwells upon images and ideas. Obviously these cognitive truths could very well inspire their practical fulfillment in daily life. But, according to the Yoga Sutras, the highest state of consciousness requires the meditator to expand his awareness beyond the operation of the discursive mind. For whatever is presented discursively is always rooted in the sensory data from which it arose. To this extent, the discursive mind cannot help but grasp its knowable objects in a conditioned, finite, incomplete fashion. Even to speak of infused contemplation as the divine bestowal of ideas or truths does not allow one to exceed the natural, internal limitations of the mind's faculties.

If there is any dependency upon the mental faculties, however subtle, the act of meditation or contemplation remains subject to the imaginative and discursive fields of finite consciousness. Even if one could still the movement of mind at the discursive level, one would then have to reckon with the surging forth of the subconsicous field. In either case, concepts and memory images occupy the mind's attention, and the transcendental state of mystic union remains only a distant yearning.

A question arises: Do the traditional theological manuals chart the processes of meditation and contemplation as these were actually performed by Christian mystics? Or, is the theoretical scrutiny of the mystics' writings restructured into the manual form to fit with certain theological presuppositions? A certain dualism is preserved and sustained in the way the manuals treat the relationship between the meditator and his goal throughout his spiritual evolution to the highest state of contemplation. Yet the mystics themselves contradict this theological presupposition. St. Teresa speaks of "an utter transformation in God." A medieval work called *Theologia Germanica* asks the question: "What is it to be a partaker of the Divine Nature, or a God-like man? He who is imbued with the Eternal or Divine Light and inflamed or consumed with Eternal or Divine Love, he is a deified man and a partaker of the Divine Nature."[29] That the notion of "deification" is not an innovative term spun out of the hallucinations of some obscure but overzealous believer is verified in similar works throughout the centuries. The church father St. Athanasius remarks in speaking of the purpose of the Incarnation of the Word of God, "He became man that we might become God."[30] In the words of Meister Eckhart, "If I am to know God directly, I must become completely He and He I, so that this He and this I become and are one I."[31] A medieval mystic, Richard of St. Victor, speaks of deification: when the soul "is plunged in the fire of divine love, like iron, it first loses its blackness, and then growing to white heat, it becomes like unto the fire itself. And lastly, it grows liquid, and losing its nature is transmuted into an utterly different quality of being."[32]

From this brief survey of mystics, the description of the ultimate attainment by those who had reached it reveals less of a duality than a unitive state of being. These meditative seekers of the transcendent absolute describe the consummation of their quest in the language of a transforming union so far above the imagination of orthodox believers as to scandalize them. While their metaphors and analogies may differ according to their cultural background, temperaments, and tastes, there is a fixed conviction running through their writings of man's latent absoluteness, expressed in a multitude of symbols. This absoluteness transcends the discursive faculties, expanding the meditator's awareness into the pure, unstructured experience of infinite consciousness. Meditation and union with reality become one. As the Christian mystic Ruysbroeck said,

> Thus do we grow and, carried above ourselves, above reason, into the very heart of love, there do we feed according to the spirit; and taking flight for the Godhead by naked love, we go to the encounter of the Bridegroom, to the encounter of His Spirit, which is His love; and thus we are brought forth by God, out of our selfhood, into the immersion of love, in which we possess blessedness and are one with God.[33]

The poetic quality of his language is distilled by the more abstract and metaphysical terminology of Patanjali, where the goal of meditation is described as self-realization. The yogic meditator, like the Christian meditator, expands to the inexhaustible state of infinite knowledge; his soul or individual consciousness is engulfed by the absolute cosmic consciousness. Certainly, in the beginning, a similar dualism appears between the yogic meditator and his experience of meditating. As the meditator continues his inner practices, a dawning intuition reveals that mind and body, spirit and matter, inner reality and outer reality are only apparently separated. What has started out as obviously dual at the sense and mental levels, recedes into an unparalleled unity at the absolute state of blissful or blessed awareness.

If one may compare the East and West as we have done, then certain revisions may be advanced. The Christian manuals' treatment of meditation is improperly limited. The imagination and discursive activity of mental prayer by its own standards retains the practitioner within the sensory and conceptual field of awareness. Reaching God or a transcendental state is prevented by the very instructions given for the activity. Christian contemplation being akin to intuition—although as the manuals understand it, still using the mental faculties—likewise keeps the aspirant from any transcendental experience. Yet the evidence of authentic transcendental states in the Christian tradition can be found by examining the lives and texts of the mystics' writings themselves. In comparison, the manuals measure their acceptable interpretation of these writings by certain psychological and theological criteria, which do not seem to do full justice to the evidence.

In view of our comparison, certain clarifications can now be made. Strictly speaking, meditation is not prayer. Prayer is generally defined as speaking to God. It, like contemplation, uses images and thoughts. Contemplation may be defined as reflection upon a particular thought or external object. Meditation, however, is essentially a non-discursive, inward journey of the mind to discover all the levels of consciousness in order to be in perfect union with them. This discovery of meditation leads to complete self-realization.

In concluding, if one accepts Underhill's definition of mysticism as "the art of union with Reality,"[34] then an unexpected convergence arises: for this definition equally spells out the meaning of yoga. It seems evident that the underlying principles of both traditions are essentially the same.

Notes

1. Epistle and Diognetum, cap. 5-6, in Pierre Pourrat, *Christian Spirituality* (Westminster, MD: Newman Press, 1953), p. 37.

2. Athanasius, Archbishop of Alexandria, "The Life of Saint Anthony," in *Stories of the Holy Fathers,* trans. Ernest A. Wallis Budge (London: Oxford University Press), pp. 10, 24.

3. Ibid., p. lxix.

4. Palladius, "The Paradise," in Budge, op. cit., pp. 193-194.

5. John Meyendorff, *St. Gregory Palamas and Orthodox Spirituality* (New York: St. Vladimir Seminary Press, 1974), pp. 36-38.

6. Palladius, op. cit., pp. 193-194.

7. St. Nikodimos and St. Makarios, *The Philokalia,* vol. 1, trans. G.E.H. Palmer, Philip Sherrard, and Kallistos Ware (London: Faber and Faber, 1979), p. 60.

8. Ibid., p. 64.

9. Ibid., p. 65.

10. Ibid., p. 68.

11. Meyendorff, op. cit., p. 24.

12. Igumen Chariton, *The Art of Prayer,* trans. E. Kadloubovsky (London: Faber and Faber, 1966), p. 77.

13. Ibid., p. 36.

14. St. Nikodimos and St. Makarios, op. cit., p. 192.

15. Pourrat, op. cit., p. 241.

16. Dionysius the Areopagite, *The Mystical Theology,* trans. C. E. Rolt (London: S.P.C.K., 1971), p. 191.

17. Richard of St. Victor, *De Exterminatione Mali,* pt. 3, chap. 18.

18. Edmund Colledge, *The Medieval Mystics of England* (New York: Sheed and Ward, 1962), pp. 137-139.

19. Julian of Norwich, *Showings,* trans. Edmund Colledge and James Walsh (New York: Paulist Press, 1978), p. 265.

20. Catherine of Sienna, *Vita e Dottrina,* cap. 18, in Evelyn Underhill, *Mysticism* (New York: Dutton, 1961), p. 441.

21. *The Book of Privy Counseling,* ed. William Johnson (New York: Image Books, 1973), pp. 156-157.

22. Pourrat, op. cit., p. 23.

23. Ignatius of Loyola, *The Spiritual Exercises,* trans. Anthony Mattola (New York: Image Books, 1964).

24. Adolphe Tanquerey, *The Spiritual Life,* trans. H. Branderis (Boston: Benziger Brothers, 1930), p. 32.

25. Antonio Royo and Jordan Aumann, *The Theology of Christian Perfection* (Dubuque, Iowa: The Priory Press, 1962), p. 514.

26. Ibid., p. 529.

27. Ibid., pp. 532-533.

28. Patanjali, *Yoga Sutras,* trans. I. K. Taimni (Wheaton, Ill.: Theosophical Publishing House, 1975), section 3.2, p. 278.

29. *Theologia Germanica,* trans. Susanna Winkworth (London: Stuart and Watkins, 1966), p. 103.

30. St. Anthanasius, *On the Incarnation of the Word Against the Nestorians,* 1:108.

31. Meister Eckhart, *Sermon 99,* in Underhill, op. cit., p. 420.

32. *De Quatuor Gradibus Violentae Charitatis in Patrologia Latina* (Paris, 1844-1855), vol. 196.

33. Ruysbroeck, *De Calculo,* in Underhill, op. cit., pp. 312-313.

34. Evelyn Underhill, *Practical Mysticism* (New York: Dutton, 1943), p. 3.

Hesychasm and the Origins of Christian Meditative Discipline

Father William Teska

The beginnings of Christian meditative discipline are very early, going back to the very origin of Christian monasticism in the third century in the desert of Egypt, and continuing over the centuries to their flowering in many places. The tradition flowered, in particular, in northern Greece during the Byzantine Empire, especially at Mount Athos. There, a school of meditation known as Hesychasm developed between the tenth and fourteenth centuries and continues down to the present day.

It is interesting for our purposes to note that the development of Christian meditative disciplines should have begun in Egypt because much of the intellectual, philosophical, and theological basis of the practice of meditation in Christianity also comes out of the theology of Hellenic and Roman Egypt. This is significant because it was in Alexandria that Christian theology had the most contact with the various gnostic speculations, which, according to many scholars, have their roots in the East, possibly in India.

There are many similarities between the systems of theology found in India and the various gnostic systems of theology, some Christian and some non-Christian, which flourished, especially in Egypt, before and shortly after the time of Christ. The idea of the transmigration of souls, for example, has an analogue in gnostic speculations originating in Greek thought. This concept was known in Pythagorean philosophy as metempsychosis, and it was absorbed by the greatest theologian of the ancient Church between St. Paul and St. Augustine—Origen of Alexandria.

Origen, who died in A.D. 255, was part of the Catechetical school in Egypt. His teacher was Clement, and Clement's teacher was a mysterious figure called Pantaenus who, according to Coptic legend, spent a good deal of his time in India. In addition to his training in this tradition, Origen had close contact with the original Christian monks in the desert outside of Alexandria. Thus, even though scholarship has yet to establish a definite link between gnosticism and ancient Indian Brahmanism, there may be such a connection because Origen's system of Christian theology drew heavily upon the gnostic traditions that were current in Egypt at his time, and many of his thoughts—indeed, his whole world view—bear striking resemblance to some of the major ideas of Hindu theology.

While it would be dangerous to assume too easily that Christianity assimilated many Hindu traditions in the manner just described, yet it is certain that the birthplace of Christian monasticism and the contemplative tradition (that is, Egypt) was also the home of those systems of Christian theology that bore the closest resemblance to Indian systems. It was in Egypt, for example, that ascetic discipline first arose in the Church (*ascesis* in Greek simply means training, athletic training as for a contest). St. Paul had already used the athletic analogy when he spoke of the Christian life as a race, and the ancient monks understood asceticism to be a very palpable type of training, physical as well as spiritual, which was best undertaken alone in the desert.

After a century or so there arose among the ascetic monks the tradition of seeking the guidance of certain spiritual fathers, analogous to masters or gurus, for it had become clear, in the development of ascetic practice, that total solitude, starting from the beginning of one's spiritual struggle, could sometimes be destructive and even diabolical. For this reason one of the greatest early ascetic theologians of the Christian East, John Klimakos, issued a very stern warning to those who would embark on a life of spiritual training or ascesis and he insisted that the first step in such a discipline was to find a spiritual father and to place oneself entirely under his guidance.

Before continuing with the description of the development of ascetic theology, it would be helpful at this point to say a few words about church history, because Americans have at best a very foggy notion about forms of Christianity other than Protestantism. Most of us, for instance, have heard of the Greek Orthodox Church or the Russian Orthodox Church, but very few of us know much about the ancient roots of the tradition. We think of Christianity as the Bible-oriented social institution that finds its expression in the numerous Protestant denominations existing in the United'States, but this form of Christianity is only a small part of the whole. It is, as it were, merely a small twig on the branch of the trunk of the whole tree that is the Christian church, and this is something quite different indeed from the type of Christianity of which we speak when we talk about the monks of ancient Egypt. This is important to note because the practices of contemplation and meditation in which we are interested were developed primarily and were most important in the Christian East.

There were in the ancient world five great centers of Christianity: Rome, Antioch, Alexandria, Constantinople, and Jerusalem, and each of these cities was the See of a patriarch, the chief bishop of the church in that part of the world. It is not our purpose here to investigate the historical and theological causes for the fact that during the Middle Ages the four Eastern patriarchs (Antioch, Alexandria, Constantinople, and Jerusalem) became increasingly estranged from the patriarch of Rome and eventually lost all communication with him; a convenient date for this split, long honored by historians, is 1054 when the pope excommunicated the patriarch of Constantinople, and the patriarch of Constantinople excommunicated the pope.

But the division started long before that with the breakdown of communication that ensued after the Gothic invasions of the Western empire. One result of this breakdown is still with us, and that is the fact that we Westerners have become extremely chauvinistic in that we know almost nothing of the development of anything in Byzantium, including Christianity. But it was there in Byzantium that the ascetic life was emphasized and the spiritual and contemplative life was developed, while in the West the emphasis quickly came to be more rational and scientific, beginning with the development of scholasticism in the twelfth and thirteenth centuries.

It is interesting to note that about the same time the scholastic movement was laying the foundations of Western science in the West, the monks of the East were beginning to develop the practice known as Hesychasm, which is remarkably similar to yoga in many ways. It was developed as a result of a long, long line of teachers (not necessarily in a direct master-disciple relationship, although there were long periods in which this was the case). Unfortunately, however, we have no reliable historical information as to the length of the continuity of such lines of masters and teachers, yet it is certain that such lines did exist, and it is interesting to notice the similarity here with Indian tradition.

It would be a great mistake to draw too many analogies between Hesychast and yoga practices, but there are, nevertheless, similarities, however superficial they may be. We know, for example, that there were periods of several centuries in which the teaching of ascetic practice passed from spiritual father to disciple, as is the case with yoga. This started in the Egyptian desert and continues to the present day, although it is often impossible to trace the succession of masters and disciples with historical accuracy. Monasteries dissolved, there were great upheavals in society, some of the practices were lost, and the tradition has not been so evenly preserved as has the tradition of yoga. But even so, tradition still exists in Christianity, and it is preserved in writing and in various other forms. There are still Hesychasts in the Holy Mountain (Athos), and in Soviet Russia.

As mentioned above, Christian meditative discipline began in ancient Egypt, and the experience of the fathers of the desert, as they are called, plays to this day an essential part in the training of Christian ascetics. (The Eastern Hesychasts, especially, view the fathers of the desert and their successors over the centuries with great reverence). The first and foremost of these was the famous Anthony. Everyone has at some time seen a painting of the temptations of St. Anthony, for this motif depicts Anthony in his warfare against spiritual adversaries, a favorite theme of medieval artists. Many other fountainheads of Christian ascetic practice could also be named here, but among the most important were Dionysius, the pseudo-Areopagite, who wrote the first treatise on mystical theology, and St. John Klimakos, mentioned above. *Klimakos* simply means "ladder," and John is so named because of his treatise on ascetic theology called *The Ladder of Divine Ascent* in which he enumerated thirty-three stages (steps on the ladder) in the progress of the soul into oneness with the Godhead.

The goal of all of the ascetic and mystical practices of Christianity was, for the ancients, nothing less than divinization. This word is seldom used in Western Christianity, but it was very important in Hellenic and Eastern Christianity. The same word in Greek is *apotheosis,* and it means "becoming one with God in an ineffable and mysterious way." Origen speaks of it, and it was so important to the fathers of the ancient church that when the church found it necessary to entertain a new doctrine or a new theological system, the question would always be raised, "Does this new teaching allow for apotheosis or not? Does it allow for humanity to become one with God?" If the new doctrine did not allow for apotheosis, it was treated with great suspicion; if it did, it was entertained. Thus, apotheosis was the ideal in ancient Eastern theology as well as the goal of ascetic discipline. Theologians such as Dionysius, the pseudo-Areopagite, and John Klimakos pursued this quest of apotheosis as did all subsequent Byzantine theologians of any importance. St. Simeon Stylites, for instance, St. Maximus the Confessor, and St. John of Damascus were all practicing ascetics, pursuing the quest of apotheosis, and this tradition continued right down to the tenth century when Hesychasm began to be important as a school of meditation.

The first great exponent of this school was a theologian named St. Simeon Neotheologos, who was so highly regarded in the East that he was called the "New Theologian" (the "First Theologian" was St. John the Divine, the writer of the Fourth

Gospel and the Apocalypse), and he is famous for having written a series of instructions to Hesychasts on the subject of mental quiet. *(Hesychia* in Greek simply means "quiet," and Hesychasm is the practice of developing this interior calm and quiet with a specific end in mind—that of apotheosis, or becoming one with God.)

Many of Simeon's instructions to Hesychasts, or those who were embarked on a life of the practice of mental quiet, are interesting because of the comparisons that can be made between them and yogic discipline. They included physical exercises (as in hatha yoga) and certain meditative postures—one of which involved sitting with the back straight and with the beard pressed against the sternum, the eyes fixed upon the abdomen. This posture gave rise to the derogatory Latin term which has come into our own language in its English translation as "navel gazer." "Sit and contemplate your navel," people say, when speaking of meditation in a derogatory way. (This was a term that the Jesuits invented for the Hesychasts because of the posture described above.) But one of the purposes of this posture is to try to fix one's attention on the location of the heart, first to become aware of the heartbeat and then to find within the breast the location of the heart. At the same time, according to Hesychasm, one's breathing is to become slow and regular, and the well-known Jesus Prayer is to be repeated many, many times like a mantra.

It is because of the importance of the heart that the discipline of Hesychasm and the particular prayer, "Lord Jesus Christ, Son of God, have mercy upon me," have become known as Prayer of the Heart. Hesychast theoreticians held that by concentrating on the heart and by breathing in a regular way (as taught by the master to the disciple) and at the same time by repeating the prayer of Jesus (or some other prayer assigned by the spiritual father), the soul could progress to ever-higher stages of consciousness and sanctity until at last it was enabled to perceive the radiance of the Godhead immediately, directly, and fully. Such a vision, of course, can be recognized as a description of the ancient goal of apotheosis, and the Hesychasts had developed what they considered to be a methodical practice to prepare oneself for this.

The practice of Hesychasm flourished mainly at a place called Mount Athos, located east of Thessalonika and west of Constantinople, which is probably the most important center of Christian spirituality since the Egyptian desert. Mount Athos, also called simply the Holy Mountain, has been a center of Christian monasticism since the ninth century, and no woman has set foot on it since that time. There are at present some twenty-eight to thirty active monasteries—Greek, Russian, Serbian, Syrian, and so on—on the holy mountain, even though it must be recognized that it is not what it once was, and there are signs of apparent decline. There were at one time, for instance, Russian monasteries built there by the imperial family in the nineteenth century, and some of the largest monasteries, called *lavras,* were, in fact, small cities that held up to three thousand monks. Almost all of these were Hesychasts.

A controversy arose during the centuries that followed the work of St. Simeon, the "New Theologian," and it culminated in the fourteenth century with the work of the great theologian, St. Gregory of Palamas. The basic question of the controversy was whether or not it is possible for a created being to perceive, without meditation, the essence of the Godhead. Could a human being, imprisoned in the body, hope to perceive the uncreated light, the light that surrounded our Lord when He was transfigured before the apostles on Mount Tabor? Could, in other words, a human being really hope to achieve apotheosis?

The Hesychast party, of course, said yes, it could be done through the disciplines of asceticism and mental quiet; that is, the disciplines of Hesychasm. The opposing party, whose intellectual leader was a certain Barlaam of Calabria, held that such a vision of God is impossible for human beings. The controversy raged, and at one point St. Gregory was deposed and imprisoned, but finally he was reinstated and made the Bishop of Thessalonika. Finally, the Hesychast party won the theological issue, and a special feast was dedicated in the Orthodox Church in honor of this victory. One may see the symbol of this victory of Hesychasm in the habit of any Orthodox monk even to this day, for on his hand he wears a string of beads, much like a rosary, which is used for counting the number of Jesus Prayers that he says under the direction of his spiritual father.

The practice of Hesychasm on Mount Athos continued up until the beginning of the nineteenth century when large numbers of Russian monks started to arrive on the holy mountain. Then from Mount Athos, the practice of Hesychasm was carried back to Russia. Those who have read *Frannie and Zooey* by J. D. Salinger have heard of the remarkable book called *The Way of the Pilgrim,* written by an anonymous Russian peasant in the nineteenth century. In it he describes his journey through Russia during which he encounters a Hesychast monk who teaches him to say the Jesus Prayer and gives him certain other exercises. With that alone, the pilgrim embarks on a life of prayer and mental quiet.

There were many such pilgrims and holy men in Russia in the nineteenth century when asceticism was still very strong, and some of the most powerful of these Hesychasts became known as *startsi,* or elders. These holy men lived in all parts of Russia (some even came to Alaska and introduced the practice to American soil), and many of them had large followings, sometimes numbered in the hundreds of thousands. Even as late as the 1930s there was a famous *starets* living on Mount Athos who wrote about his own spiritual pilgrimage, and whose life was a fine example of Eastern piety—in particular, of Hesychasm.

The Russian revolution forced a great many vital spiritual traditions underground. Even so, although it is very difficult to say with any certainty whether the tradition of Hesychasm is still strong in Russia, it may be assumed that there are still practitioners, because Hesychasm played such an important role in Russian spirituality at its deepest level. On Mount Athos there are still hermits and ascetics, some of whom live in caves and who can be visited only by climbing up chains to the part of the cliff in which they live. They hardly ever see anyone, but it is more than likely that they still practice the ancient disciplines.

Jesus and Meditation

Arpita, Ph.D.

The teachings of Jesus conveyed in the Gospels constitute, in essence, a manual for meditation. In figurative language they describe the various stages of meditation, provide guidelines for overcoming obstacles in practice, and explain the ultimate outcome of the meditative endeavor. At face value, the Gospels provide instruction in ethics and set forth a philosophy of love and service, but at the allegorical and transcendental levels their symbolic meaning can be apprehended and applied to enhance spiritual growth through the practice of meditation. Here meditation is defined not as prayer or contemplation or dialogue with the divine but as the complete control of mind and purity of heart that lead to the realization of oneness with the Absolute Consciousness.

Such control and purity are attained by constant regular practice of intense loving concentration on the divine over a long period of time. This leads to the state known as enlightenment, sainthood, Self-realization, heaven, or the kingdom of God. Meditation pierces through the realm of sensation, emotion, thought, discourse, image, intuition, and ecstasy to the unalloyed realm of one-pointed identification with the spirit. The salvation or conversion experience spoken of in the Christian tradition is but one possible turning point on the path to Self-realization or heaven. Meditation is a practical and simple method of spiritual practice that transcends era, culture, and religion. All the great religions of the world have utilized some method of meditation, each with its own identifying but nonessential embellishments unique to the background of those who developed it. The meditative tradition itself is universal, because the practice of meditation is an intrinsic aspect of human nature.

The Yoga Sutras of Patanjali systematically describe, in a precise and straightforward manner, the nature of meditation, its results, and its ultimate purpose. From the perspective of this ancient authoritative text, the life of Jesus is an excellent representation of the qualities that characterize the highest meditative state, for the results of such practice are readily evident in his character. His keen intellect, steady equanimity, selfless love and service, complete nonattachment, special powers, profound philosophy, fearlessness, conviction, and spiritual perfection are the hallmarks of attainment in meditation. Although no specific mention that Jesus actually practiced a particular method of meditation is found in the orthodox Christian canon, the Gospels do describe half a dozen situations in which Jesus slipped away to some quiet solitary place for spiritual practice. The nature of such practice is not described, nor are the techniques that he must have conveyed to his close disciples, whose teachings and characters also reflect a meditative influence.

Jesus initiated only a few chosen ones into his higher teachings, saying to his disciples, "The secret of the kingdom of God is given to you, but to those who are outside, everything comes in parables" (Mark 4:11). It is evident that Jesus never intended to impart the higher teachings to the general audience, but rather meant to convey them privately only to the few who were prepared and earnest. To the general public he gave basic ethical norms and inspiring lessons: "Jesus spoke to the crowds in parables; indeed, he would never speak to them except in parables" (Matt. 13:34). But to his close disciples he imparted the depths of his wisdom and the practical aspects of his teachings: "He spoke the word to them [the crowds] as far as they were capable of understanding it . . . but he explained everything to his disciples when they were alone" (Mark 4:33-34). Even from among the apostles, only Peter, James, and John were given more advanced teachings, and of all his students, only the John of Revelation was prepared to realize the truth in its entirety.

The evangelists and Paul addressed the bulk of their writings only to the general layperson; thus the orthodox canon contains little instruction in higher practices for the advanced and devoted practitioner. The few gospel sayings—such as are found in the Sermon on the Mount—that Jesus directed to his close disciples are truly understood only on a transcendental level by those prepared students who have developed "ears to hear" (Matt. 11:15, Mark 4:9). Jesus conveyed his message through the medium of poetry because the profundity of the Truth is too complex for prose—the real meaning is gleaned beyond the realm of language.

Because Jesus' sayings are cloaked in allegory and because his own practices are not described, modern seekers who turn to the teachings of Jesus for guidance in spiritual practice must prepare themselves so they are able to read into the depth of his words with the discriminating eye of the heart, which goes beyond the literal message spoken for the masses. Then they must listen with the spiritual ear to hear the message within and beyond. The metaphor provides a filtering system for the teacher. It is a test of the student's level of preparedness because those who have no inner experience or awareness cannot suspect its deeper meaning. Those who can, deserve further instruction, for only those on the shadowy brink of discerning a truth for themselves can realize and assimilate it through the teacher's timely instruction.

It is traditional for a realized teacher to pass on the heritage of the tradition to a qualified student orally and in private. Written records of the highest teachings are never made; they are passed on individually through oral instruction, practice, and even silence. Cryptic, symbolic representations of basic concepts is all that is written or drawn. Jesus kept his true teachings hidden beneath the guise of metaphor so that those who had not already had some inner experience would not understand his language. He did not want to "give to dogs what is holy or throw [his] pearls before swine" because they would have no way of understanding his true meaning and would "trample" it (Matt. 7:6). The yogic scriptures similarly caution teachers to instruct only those who have prepared themselves through intense inner work, warning, "Do not impart; do not impart."

Two Distinct Systems: Jesus and Christianity

The teachings of Jesus were never organized and codified into a practical and comprehensive system of spiritual development, as were the yogic teachings by Patanjali in the Yoga Sutras. This is in part due to the fact that no record of his specific practices was available and in part because the proper interpretation and application of the readily accessible teachings were not known. Recently, however, additional fragments of early Christian texts have been discovered that shed a bit more light on Jesus' system by describing some specific meditative practices and spiritual teachings. These ancient Christian scriptures—the Nag Hammadi Library and the Dead Sea Scrolls—are early Gnostic and Essene writings that fill in many gaps regarding the practical aspects of Jesus' teachings. They were apparently deleted from the official canon and suppressed by the early Church in an attempt to hone the Christian teachings down to a level most easily acceptable to a majority of people. For as the young Christian Church grew, ecclesiastical necessity dictated the creation of a single doctrine designed for the masses. The Church is for the many, and its canon has to be palatable to the many, not just the few. The most subtle and profound concepts and the most demanding and advanced techniques of Jesus' teachings were only for the prepared few. They were therefore not provided to the average layperson, and through the years even the clergy lost contact with these teachings. By A.D. 367, the scriptures describing these teachings had been marked as heretical and destroyed; their oral tradition eventually became disused and also vanished.

Not only were records of the actual practices and concepts missing, but the mode for conceptualizing such teachings as they are figuratively described in the extant scriptures was eventually lost as well. Philosophical frameworks are described through the medium of language, and the limitations of this medium shape their structure. Jesus worked with language as an artist would, stretching and redefining its capacity; it is a major challenge to translate such a delicate and precise construct through era, culture, language, and levels of consciousness. Furthermore, the Scriptures of modern Christianity are largely based on translations of translations, and the message they convey has thus been molded and remolded by the cultural influences and linguistic restrictions of various times and places. Their accuracy (especially the King James Version) is therefore disputable. The English-language version of the Bible is able to deal only with certain concepts, and it carries with it a load of connotation-weighted words—such as *God, repent, sin, hell, temptation,* and *salvation*—that could alter Jesus' original intent. These value-laden terms reflect later interpretations of the original teaching, and they have strong emotional effects on followers, negatively shading their views of life. This may serve to keep the lower urges at bay and maintain social order, but it distorts the emotions, hardens the ego, and contracts the mind, and thus it is not spiritual. Jesus taught devotion and service, not rules and threats; but Christianity frequently uses fear and guilt as motivators rather than emphasizing the love and spirituality of its founder.

Although the basic philosophy that Jesus conveyed can still be discerned, his higher philosophical tenets and the systematic procedures that he taught for attaining Christ-consciousness have been lost, misunderstood, fragmented, and diluted. This high level of teachings is experiential, not didactic, and it is not possible for a religion to teach this en masse, or even to guarantee its perpetuation among the elite. The thread of such an oral tradition is easily lost because it depends not on structure and formulas but on the spiritual attainment of individuals. It is readily apparent that the philosophy of Jesus is quite distinctly different from and more highly advanced than the philosophy of Christianity. These are clearly two different systems. In the course of time, however, the basic ethical code and the ritual and dogma formulated by the Church centuries after Jesus imparted his message eventually became identified as the accepted method of practicing the teachings of Jesus. But Jesus did not teach merely a social or moral system; he taught a spiritual one. Such degeneration of teachings to the lowest common denominator seems to be the fate of all great systems as they become popular—the weight of time and numbers crushes the deeper message of the enlightened founder.

Bureaucratic structure and organized religion cannot carry the profound and delicate wonders of the spiritual experience. At best they can encourage hope and morality among the masses, but all too often they create fear, rigidity, and conflict instead. A religious tradition is something different from a spiritual tradition. Religion is cultural and societal, but spirituality is universal and individual. Saints and sages impart spiritual knowledge; churches and clergy preach religion. Religions are like many varied boxes, all containing the same one essence of spirituality. Many followers cling to the package only, not realizing the richness it holds. They mistake the container for the contents. The box can be a means to recognize and enjoy the contents, but it can also be a barrier that perpetuates division and ignorance.

Jesus himself never endorsed the rigid practices and theories of organized religion, and in fact he eschewed all signs of "Churchianity." The path of worship he pointed out was based on inner experience and was to be followed by each individual in privacy and silence. Although the orthodox Christian churches may not be able to convey Jesus' full message, his lineage is yet carried on by means of an invisible inner church, for it seems that there are two streams of tradition that flow from the teachings Jesus conveyed: the orthodox church and the hidden internal path. These can and, with some, do co-exist, but they usually do not. For clarity, let us compare and contrast them.

The orthodox church, which crystallized in the second to the fourth centuries A.D., is an external, visible, public institution with specific rituals and trappings, and a fixed creed, dogma, clerical heirarchy, and political structure. Membership is by baptism, and initiation is by ordination. The Church claims exclusive authority to teach, and adherents are instructed that the way to know God is to follow the teachings of the Church. Church dogma is therefore geared to the many, and so it must be accessible, unanimous, and literal, and must establish and uphold social harmony. A basic ethical code and an inspirational message are thus paramount, and seeking for knowledge beyond the established rule and dogma is not encouraged. It is even thought of as potentially dangerous, for it is believed that there is nothing to be known beyond the accepted recognized teachings, and to question their validity threatens one's only access to the divine—the Church. The cosmology of the Church is monotheistic and dualistic, and that which separates the individual from God is said to be sin or evil. God, through the Church, is responsible for saving that believer who obeys the tenets of the faith and adheres to its moral code. Members can thereby enjoy the eternal bliss of heaven after death, and a few can attain sainthood.

The internal tradition, on the other hand, is invisible, individual, personal, and secret. There are no recognizable signs, rules, creeds, or rituals. It has existed throughout all times and cultures, but as an enlightened one, Jesus was a source of that tradition, and many within it accept him as their divine guide. Membership in the internal tradition is through spiritual experience, and initiation is through grace bestowed to deserving and prepared practitioners. There is no formal structure, and authority comes from inner attainment. Instruction is oral, from the accomplished teacher to the sincere student, and the words of the great teachers are accepted on a symbolic and transcendental level as understood through inner perception. The major way to knowledge, however, is to know oneself from within; the individual is responsible for his or her own realization, and no external source can bestow it. This tradition is conveyed internally—guidance is from within. The way of practice is silent, solitary, ascetic, and inner-seeking. No specific formulas are ordered, but perseverence in discovering oneself on all levels is thought to be essential to realize the divinity within. Ignorance is seen as the cause of an individual's apparent separation from the divine, and it is this illusion which causes suffering. The cosmology is monistic—rather than becoming Christian, practitioners become Christ through realizing their Christ-consciousness while still alive.

The Gnostic and Essene traditions were philosophically

more aligned with the orientation of the inner church, but the orthodox tradition apparently prevailed over these. Modern orthodox Christianity has yet to officially recognize the newly discovered Gnostic and Essene scriptures, and most Christians do not know them. For these reasons, their contents—though of immense value, if only to show how little is really understood of Jesus' teachings—will not be discussed here, and the focus will remain on the teachings conveyed allegorically in the orthodox Scriptures. The philosophy of the internal church can yet be gleaned from them in this way. Jesus' gospel sayings represent his cosmology most accurately, and despite the barriers of language and time, they paint a shimmeringly clear picture of his views, if one perceives them with care and openness to see their hidden essence.

The philosophy of Jesus can be compared philosophically to the Eastern systems of Yoga or Vedanta, but historical Christianity is more similar to historical Buddhism. Christianity's aim is to rise above mere materialism and to reduce suffering, but the aims of Yoga and Jesus are more positive and spiritual than this—they show the way to realize one's union with divinity. Jesus' philosophy is similar to Eastern philosophies in many ways, but the outstanding aspect is the use of meditation. This essential spiritual practice has been lost in the orthodox Christian traditions, which practice contemplation, concentration, prayer, and ritual, but not meditation as it is defined in Eastern systems.

In an effort to enrich the impoverished methodology of the Christian meditative tradition, many modern Christian writers—such as Thomas Merton, William Johnston, Dom Aelred Graham, Bede Griffiths, and Jacob Needleman (with his mysterious Father Sylvan)—have been attempting to piece together and revive a method of meditative practice useful for clergy and laity alike. The early Church turned to the West and was strongly influenced by its logical and mechanistic orientation, but such modern Christian writers are currently investigating the Eastern orientation and applying its methods of meditation to the Christian context. Thus they are reformulating what Father

Sylvan calls an intermediate level of spiritual practice, a level that provides the means for following a spiritual path that will result in the establishment of virtue and the realization of one's union with the divine. It is this that orthodox Christianity has lost, though it is an essential aspect of Jesus' teachings.

The Method of Practice

Only a few rare individuals, by strength of their own ardor and sincerity, have attained this high state of divine realization, and they have done so from within. Many Christian saints have practiced meditation, and have followed their inner teacher—Jesus—not the Church. It is they—not the ecclesiastical hierarchy—and those who have sought Christ-consciousness through Jesus—not dogma and ritual—who have carried on the real tradition of Jesus. Their path is internal, as is their spiritual initiation. Many saints have been in open opposition to the Church, many have worked to reform it, and some have even been excommunicated or executed as heretics. The nature of sainthood and the way to attain it is neither understood nor taught, and mysticism is often viewed with skepticism. Many modern Christians actually doubt the possibility of realizing the kingdom of God in this lifetime, assuming that heaven is to be attained by the virtuous few only after death. Jesus, however, proclaimed the attainment of divine perfection in this lifetime as the ultimate goal for his followers.

Jesus proclaimed this essential teaching: "The kingdom of God is within you" (Luke 17:21). And he instructed his apostles, "Be thou perfect, even as thy Father in heaven is perfect" (Matt. 5:48); "I tell you truly, there are some standing here who will not taste death before they see the kingdom of God" (Luke 9:27). Realization of the divine perfection dwelling within is heaven, and it is to be attained now—before death.

With this as the stated goal for his disciples, Jesus' task was to instruct them in the means for attaining it. So he told them, "When you pray, go into your room, shut the door, and pray to your Father who is hidden. Your Father, who sees what is hidden, will reward you. And when you pray, don't use a lot of empty words" (Matt. 6:6-7). Privacy, silence, inwardness, and simplicity are suggested. And again he said, "Come away to a lonely place; rest for a time" (Mark 6:31). This is reminiscent of the Old Testament instruction to "Be still and know that I am God" (Psalm 46:10). Solitude, stillness, and a putting aside of all concerns and discomforts are the recommendations for realizing the hidden Reality within.

Jesus further states, "It is not those who say to me, 'Lord, Lord,' who will enter the kingdom of heaven" (Matt. 7:21). Mental yearning and verbal aspiration are not enough; the aspirant's actions must demonstrate deep inner conviction and willingness to go deeper. He must be worthy—that is, sincere, concentrated, gentle, and faithful from within. Superficial devotional practices and external methods of worship are mere nonessential trappings. "God is spirit, and those who worship must worship in spirit and truth" (John 4:24). In these instructions, Jesus seems to be telling his followers simply to focus inwardly on the spiritual reality in a state of relaxation and peace and in an atmosphere of solitude and quiet. These guidelines are the same as those given in all methods of meditation, regardless of the cultural frills that are super-imposed upon them.

If meditation does not consist of externals, then how does one practice it? Jesus taught a "message of peace" (Luke 19:42); he came "to guide our feet in the way of peace" (Luke 1:79). He told his disciples simply, "Peace be with you" (John 20:19); "Set your hearts on [the Father's] kingdom" (Matt. 6:33). Paul explains "The peace of God, which passes all understanding, will keep your hearts and thoughts" (Phil. 4:7). The mind and emotions are calmed and focused by allowing awareness of the divine presence residing beyond them to become paramount. Thought and emotion cannot effect transformation to a state of peace—only spirit can. Paul conveyed a subtle phenomenon when he said, "We do not know how to pray as we should, but the Spirit himself prays in us with a yearning which cannot be said in words" (Romans 8:26). The value of silence and of relying on the divine within that emanates from beyond the superficial mental level is described here. The concept that the doer is not the conscious mind or the individual personality is also expressed (as it is also, repeatedly, in the Bhagavad Gita, the great synthesizing text of Indian philosophy).

When Jesus' disciples specifically asked him to teach them how to pray, he told them not to ask for things but to repeat a prayer that is today referred to as the Lord's Prayer (Matt. 6:9-13). These few phrases invoke the deity (addressed intimately as *"Abba,"* which means "Father") to guide the aspirant in the way of the spirit. It is remarkably similar to the *gayatri* mantra of the Vedas, which is prescribed as a meditative focus for the purpose of purifying and strengthening the aspirant and leading him or her steadfastly to the Absolute. This mantra is given as a special beginning-level practice through initiation by a teacher, just as Jesus gave the Lord's Prayer to his chosen disciples before he revealed the full truth to them.

In addition to giving his disciples the Lord's Prayer during the Sermon on the Mount, Jesus also gave them the Golden Rule (Matt. 7:12) and described the Beatitudes to them (Matt. 5:3-12). These guidelines express certain attitudes or spiritual stances that are helpful attributes to cultivate in conjunction with one's practice. The Yoga Sutras contain a similar set of guidelines, called the *yamas* and *niyamas,* which are seen as essential behavioral and conceptual adjuncts to meditative practice. Their purpose is to reduce any environmental and emotional upset in one's life that may be distracting to effective spiritual endeavor. Peter addressed the same issue, saying, "Leave all ill-will, bad feeling, slander, and jealousy. Like newly born babies, long for that pure spiritual milk you need to grow towards salvation; because you have tasted the Lord's kindness" (1 Peter 2:1-3). Interpersonal disruptions are obstacles to practice (i.e. "sin"); conversely, one is benefited by shifting one's focus to the positive and by yearning for divinity with a feeling of trust and gratitude. This receptive devotional quality is described in kundalini yoga as being related to the throat center, symbolized by the infant suckling milk from its mother's breast.

The Teacher and the Path

Having embarked on the spiritual journey through practicing meditation, the student encounters various difficulties that only one who has already traveled that path can guide him or her through. The teacher is a guide who has reached the ultimate goal and who offers his services to help seekers find their ways to the realization of the divine as well. Jesus taught "with authority" (Matt. 7:29) because he remained in constant awareness of the ultimate Truth. He was thus able to proclaim, "I am the Way, the Truth, and the Life: no one can come to the Father except through me" (John 14:6); "My teaching is not from myself: it comes from the one who sent me" (John 7:16); "I am the gate" (John 10:9); "I am the good shepherd" (John 10:11). The teacher is a messenger, an intermediary, a channel to the ultimate Truth. He selects his students and shows them the way. The guidance of a teacher, or *gurudeva,* is seen as essential in the yogic tradition if the student is to advance very much in meditative practice. "Gurudeva" means "that bright being who removes the darkness of ignorance." Jesus told his disciples, "I am the light of the world: anyone who follows me will not be walking in the dark; he will have the light of life" (John 8:12).

The enlightened teacher has the capacity to transform the prepared student, just as Jesus transformed the fishermen and Mary Magdalene. Jesus did not hesitate to inform his listeners that he possessed this power, as the following passages clearly illustrate: "He that believes in me has everlasting life" (John 6:47); "I am the living bread which has come down from heaven: Anyone who eats this bread will live forever" (John 6:51). Through initiation by the teacher, the student is given direct experience of the divine reality and is accepted into a tradition that provides specific means for attaining realization on one's own. Jesus said, "If any man is thirsty, let him come to me . . . and drink" (John 7:37); "Anyone who drinks the water that I shall give will never be thirsty again: the water that I shall give will turn into a spring inside him, welling up to eternal life" (John 4:14).

In the Bhagavad Gita, Krishna expressed a similar philosophy, indicating that whenever the times were evil and the world in need of help, he would manifest to provide assistance and show the way to Truth (chapter 4, verse 8). But he also indicated that no matter which path people walk, they eventually come to him, the divine (chapter 4, verse 11). The "way" is the teaching, the guidance, and the grace of an enlightened sage. It is not simply the dogma of a specific religion. There are many paths but only one goal. A definite path is needed, however, to keep one focused and to guide one safely to the goal, because the full truth cannot be realized without some method of practice or a teacher and a tradition to provide guidance and instruction. It is the rare aspirant, indeed, who attains the highest state without such guidance, for the path is narrow and the dangers many.

The Call and the Response

It has been illustrated that Jesus' instructions in how to pray are similar to the techniques described for meditation in the yoga tradition. Both emphasize solitude, silence, relaxation, turning inward, disregarding distractions, going beyond mind and emotion, and focusing on the divinity within. But Jesus gave more specific instructions to those who had deeper interest and who wanted to dedicate their lives to pursuing his guidelines to attain divine perfection. The call to the spiritual path is an inner experience that was manifested externally when Jesus chose his disciples. He recognized these few and selected them to be trained to receive the highest teachings. He said, "I know my own and my own know me" (John 10:14). The seeker recognizes the appropriate path and teacher, just as the teacher recognizes those students to whom the teachings are to be imparted. This is a reciprocal occurrence, for the student must first acknowledge and accept the inner call and then must also respond to being selected, "For many are called, but few are chosen" (Matt. 20:16). Jesus informed his disciples that "You did not choose me; no, I chose you" (John 15:16) and that "My choice withdrew you from the world" (John 15:19).

The chosen ones were called to an ascetic, disciplined way of life, a constant striving for divine union and perfection, and a complete transformation of character. The manner of responding to the call indicates the student's preparedness to tread the path. When Jesus called his disciples to "Follow me" (Matt. 9:9), no hesitation or excuse was acceptable. The call to the spiritual path requires an immediate response of clear and firm commitment; it requires full acceptance and surrender. Jesus told them, "If anyone wants to be a follower of mine, let him renounce himself and take up his cross and follow me" (Matt. 16:24, Mark 8:34, Luke 9:23). No delays, desires, or worries can be held on to; for mundane concerns—no matter how compelling—sabotage the essential inner attitude of renunciation. "Follow me, and leave the dead to bury the dead" (Matt. 8:22). The pull of the past is to be released entirely. "Once the hand is laid on the plow, no one who looks back is fit for the kingdom of God" (Luke 9:62). Family ties are also to be loosed. Jesus declared to them that "Anyone who prefers father or mother to me is not worthy of me. Anyone who prefers son or daughter to me is not worthy of me" (Matt. 10:37); "If any man comes to me without hating his father, mother, wife, children, brothers, sisters, yes, and his own life too, he cannot be my disciple" (Luke 14:26). A total shift in focus away from the temporal and mundane and toward the universal and spiritual is necessary to realize the Truth. Jesus told his inner circle of followers that they were not to think "in man's way" (Matt. 16:23) but to view life from the perspective of the divine. And he assured them that "Anyone who finds his life will lose it; anyone who loses his life for my sake will find it" (Matt. 10:39). The apostles, acting on faith, "left everything and followed him" (Luke 5:11).

This same zeal of determination and renunciation is characteristic of all meditative traditions, and only a few from among the masses are selected or prepared to follow fully. Once one has set foot on the path, one does not yield to doubt or to distractions from the past or from worldly affairs. The same is true of one's mental focus during the actual practice of meditation. Although one still has duties to perform in the world and although thoughts still arise and pass by, one is not disturbed by them in meditation. One allows these impressions to flow through, but has no interest in them and remains steadfastly concentrated on the divine. No other desires or duties supersede this primary focus of life. Paul clarifies this: "You must give up your old way of life" (Eph. 4:22); "The one thing I do is this: I forget what is in my past and strain forward to the future, to the prize of the call God gives us to move upward" (Phil. 3:13-14); "So get rid of all the old yeast, and make yourselves into a completely new batch of bread" (1 Cor. 5:7). Nonattachment to memories and to the emotions they conjure up, to worldly objects and relationships, and to old limited self-concepts is essential to the effective practice of meditation as described by Jesus and by the ancient yogic texts.

Preparation for Treading the Path

Having decided to embark on the path, one's first task is to "prepare a way for the Lord" (Matt. 3:3), to "make a straight way for the Lord" (John 1:23). If the mind is to be made still and clear enough to be capable of allowing the higher teaching to enter, there must be a period of inner purification. Jesus said, "Clean the inside of the cup and dish first so that the outside may become clean as well" (Matt. 23:26). This cleansing is done internally because "from the heart come evil intentions. . . . These are the things that make a man unclean" (Matt. 15:19-20). To cleanse within, one has to turn within, and the method for turning within, knowing oneself, releasing hidden thoughts and feelings, and finding the true center of one's being, is called meditation.

The progressive steps in turning more deeply inward are described by Jesus: "Ask, and it will be given to you; search, and you will find; knock, and the door will be opened to you: for the one who asks always receives; the one who searches always finds; the one who knocks will always have the door opened to him" (Matt. 7:7-8). These words echo Jeremiah: "Then when you call to me, and come to plead with me, I will listen to you. When you seek me, you shall find me, when you seek me with all your heart" (Jer. 29:12-13). It is the "voice of one calling in the wilderness" (Matt.

3:3, John 1:23) that is heard, responded to, and sought with unyielding persistence. One attains the goal through one-pointed striving and perseverance. Just as, in Jesus' parable, the person who knocks upon his friend's door at midnight will not stop pounding until he is given the food he needs (Luke 11:5-8), so the meditator maintains practicing until the ultimate goal is attained.

John the Baptist called out to the unbaptized to "repent" (Matt. 3:2), and Jesus also preached this (Matt. 4:17), especially to those who questioned him (Luke 13:3, 5). This injunction is not an encouragement toward penance and guilt, but it is rather a call to make a radical change in one's consciousness, to adopt a broader paradigm, leave old habit patterns, and begin afresh. As Paul states it, "You must put aside your old self. . . . Your mind must be renewed by a spiritual revolution so that you can put on the new self that has been created in God's way" (Eph. 4:22, 24). This is the way to prepare oneself to be able to receive the teachings, for as Jesus said, "Nobody puts new wine into old wineskins . . . No! new wine, fresh skins" (Mark 2:22). Paul similarly admonishes, "Do not model yourselves on the behavior of the world around you, but let your behavior change, modeled by your new mind" (Romans 12:2); "Let your thoughts be on heavenly things and not on the things that are on the earth" (Col. 3:2). This is the way to build one's house on a firm foundation. For all worldy things are transient; only the heavenly and spiritual are eternal and unchanging. Jesus said, "It is the spirit that gives life, the flesh has nothing to offer" (John 6:63). Thus Paul cries out to the unaware, "Wake up from your sleep, rise from the dead" (Eph. 5:14).

In order to progress and receive from above, one has to make oneself a worthy, capable vessel; one must make sincere efforts to decondition, reprogram, and train oneself so that one will have the capacity to comprehend the higher levels. Jesus told his followers, "You must be born from above" (John 3:7). A spiritual orientation full of trust and love is needed, and Jesus warned them, "I tell you solemnly, unless you change and become like little children, you will never enter the kingdom of heaven" (Matt. 18:3); "Anyone who does not welcome the kingdom of God like a little child will never enter it" (Mark 10:15). The qualities of little children—such as innocence, spontaneity, joy, and openness—are essential, but some adult qualities—such as doubt, egoism, defensiveness, and inflexibility—prohibit realization. The mind of a child is fresh, like the unhabituated beginner's mind much extolled in the Buddhist tradition. In yoga, such a mind free from disturbing and limiting thought patterns is developed through the persistent practice of meditation.

Focusing on the Divine Within

In turning within and purifying the mind to make a smooth and direct pathway to the divine, it is essential to have a point of focus so the mind and emotions will not wander. That focus must be within, for as Jesus said, "Know this: the kingdom of God is within you" (Luke 17:21). The importance of focusing the mind on the divine within is also reiterated throughout Paul's writings. It was he who said, "Your body is the temple of the Holy Ghost which is in you" (1 Cor. 6:19). To realize the inner dweller, however, the grosser levels of mind and body must be stilled, for they draw one's attention to the external. Jesus told his disciples, "Peace I bequeath to you; my own peace I give you; a peace the world cannot give, this is my gift to you" (John 14:27); "Peace be with you. . . . Receive the Holy Ghost" (John 20:21, 22). Peace is the prerequisite for receiving the wisdom of the Holy Spirit, and it is only divine peace—the peace of the teacher, of the Word, of the spirit—that can truly calm the heart and mind. The "peace of God," which exists beyond the conscious mind, is that which brings awareness. Jesus speaks of this inner awareness, saying, "I will ask the Father, and he will send you another Counselor, who will be with you forever. He is the Spirit of truth. . . . You know him: he lives in you" (John 14:16-17).

Jesus further instructed his apostles that "When the Spirit of truth comes he will lead you to the complete truth" (John 16:13). When the mind is finally stilled and focused inward, then one realizes the divine and consequently understands all. Everything becomes known to one whose mind is at peace, "for there is nothing hid, except to be made manifest. Nor is anything secret, except to come to light" (Mark 4:22). Jesus explained the way to attain this state, saying, "Set your mind on God's kingdom and justice, and all the rest will come to you as well" (Matt. 6:33). And Paul states that "The kingdom of God . . . means righteousness and peace and joy brought by the Holy Spirit" (Rom. 14:17). When one stills the thoughts and emotions by focusing on the peace of the divine within, one obtains complete knowledge of the Truth; then all questions are answered and all desires are fulfilled. Peace is found by turning inward and concentrating one-pointedly on the perfect peace of the divine.

Paul explains the subsequent expansion of consciousness in this way: "Now we are seeing a dim reflection in a mirror; but then we shall be seeing face to face. The knowledge that I have now is imperfect; but then I shall know as fully as I am known" (1 Cor. 13:12). Direct realization of the inner Truth reveals full and perfect understanding of all that is. Thus seeking knowledge through turning inward rather than through gathering and analyzing external data reflects an Eastern rather than a Western philosophical orientation. This is the perspective of Jesus, but the later Church developed a model that is more Western in nature.

Yoga, of course, shares Jesus' Eastern philosophical viewpoint; it is inner oriented. Patanjali, the codifier of the Yoga Sutras, said, "Yoga is the control of thought-waves in the mind. Then man abides in his real nature" (book 1, sutras 2, 3). Meditation leads to the stillness of mind in which one can clearly see one's own divine nature. But one must have an inner beacon to calm, focus, and guide the mind so it will clear and allow the light to shine through. Jesus said, "The light of the body is the eye; if therefore thine eye be single, thy whole body shall be full of light" (Matt. 6:22). He further stated, "I am the light of the world: anyone who follows me will not be walking in the dark; he will have the light of life" (John 8:12).

Praying in the Heart

Peter suggests a specific point for inner focus, saying, "Simply reverence the Lord Christ in your hearts" (1 Peter 3:15).

This method was practiced and developed more fully by the Desert Fathers of the early Church. It is essential to the hesychastic meditative method, which uses the uninterrupted "prayer of the heart," or the Jesus Prayer, described in the *Philokalia* and *The Way of a Pilgrim*. The heart as a focal point of self-understanding and divine concentration is a familiar concept in the Old Testament also. Moses cautioned his followers to know themselves by taking "heed to thyself that there be not a secret thing in thine heart" (Deut. 15:9). David likewise stated, "I spent all night meditating in my heart" (Psalm 77:6). The divine within is described in the phrase, "He has set eternity in the heart of man" (Eccles. 3:11). Finding the heart—the essential core of one's being beyond mind and emotion—and residing there is a profound spiritual practice in itself.

Paul states, "The proof that you are sons is that God has sent the spirit of his Son into our hearts" (Gal. 4:6). Jesus instructed his students, "Do not let your hearts be troubled or afraid" (John 14:27), and he told them, "Blessed are the pure in heart, for they shall see God" (Matt. 5:8). This Beatitude indicates that when the heart is purified, one can perceive one's true nature, which is divine. It is strikingly similar to Patanjali's Yoga aphorisms, which state that when the mind is emptied of thought-waves, the seer can realize his own divine nature (book 1, sutras 2, 3). Knowledge of the divine, of the Self, is gained by looking within, for it resides within every human heart. The *Kathopanishad* refers to the divine dwelling within the heart as a smokeless, unflickering flame, and kundalini yoga describes a subtle heart center, or *chakra,* as the fourth level of human consciousness. The Sacred Heart of Jesus, aflame and open, signifies the compassion and selfless outpouring of love and service that the heart chakra depicts. This center is the inner chamber, the holy tabernacle or sanctuary where the divine resides within every human shrine. It is frequently prescribed as a focus for meditation in the yogic tradition, and it is said to be the source of the *anahata nada*—the "unstruck sound"—that emanates from the silence of one's divine essence. This silent sound of the spiritual heart is heard in stillness, and it leads the aspirant to the divine within.

Paul summarizes the process of finding knowledge within in the following prayer: "Out of his infinite glory may he give you the power through his Spirit for your hidden self to grow strong so that Christ may live in your hearts through faith, and then, planted in love and built on love, you will with all the saints have strength to grasp the breadth and length, the height and depth until, knowing the love of Christ, which is beyond all knowledge, you are filled with the utter fullness of God" (Eph. 3:16-19). The Spirit has the power to transform through love so that the seeker's inner self expands, knows all, and is constantly and thouroughly of the divine within and without.

Journey Through the Unconscious

The instructions, then, are to "launch out into the deep" (Luke 5:4), which is within, and to go through the darkness, seeking the light until it is found. Practitioners are cautioned that the way will not be easy, however. Embarking on the journey within entails confronting all of one's inner conflicts, repressed memories, unmet potentials, and hidden fears that have been stored in the subconscious mind. "Everything that is now covered will be uncovered, and everything now hidden will be made clear" (Matt. 10:26).

The lower ego has a tremendous investment in defending against awareness of its hidden barriers, but they must be overcome and put to rest if one is to expand one's consciousness and make the mind still enough to be aware of the divinity within. Jesus verifies this phase, saying in figurative language, "It is not peace I have come to bring but a sword. For I have come to set a man against his father. . . . A man's enemies will be those of his own household" (Matt. 10:34-36). In the battle within, the seeker must confront intimate and deeply ingrained habits and cherished beliefs with the cold sword of discrimination. This is the same plight that Arjuna, the hero of the Bhagavad Gita, finds himself in as he confronts the members of his own family on the battlefield. All attachments must be severed, all compulsions loosed. In the bright light of truth one must dispel those thoughts that are illusory, binding, and misleading, regardless of one's attachment to them. Jesus warned his close disciples that they would have to suffer and be persecuted for the sake of following him; that is, for treading the inward path. The external world, as well as the senses and ego, resists efforts to forge inward beyond the familiar realm of matter and thought to the realm of pure consciousness and spirit. But it is this very realm alone, which is called the kingdom of God or heaven, that gives true peace.

The times of difficulty in spiritual practice are described figuratively in the story of the destruction of Jerusalem (Matthew 24, Mark 13, Luke 21) and in the entire Book of Revelation, which is itself a description of the evolution of consciousness. In the practice of meditation one learns to remain unaffected and one-pointedly focused on the divine as one allows the repressed materials of the unconscious mind to pass through and eventually be dissipated. The process of making the unconscious conscious entails the surrender of defense mechanisms that have been habitually and subliminally employed to protect the ego from emotionally charged and personally incompatible contents. Because the ego has not been able to cope with them, these repressed and suppressed materials have been assiduously relegated to and maintained in the unconscious mind. Allowing these specters hidden in the dusky corners of the mind to surface to the light of truth can be a distressful and arduous process. Thus Jesus warned his students of conflict, deception, and suffering, for one's defenses will struggle to maintain their foothold. The defense mechanisms were designed to protect us from realizations harmful to the ego's identity, but as the personality grows and strengthens, they are no longer needed. When they become barriers to further growth, they must be torn down and the fears they protected released. "The time will come when not a single stone will be left on another: everything will be destroyed" (Luke 21:6). This process of internal renewal can be painful, for one is relinquishing old coping techniques and confronting old fears, but as Paul reminds the Jews, "The Lord trains the ones he loves, and he punishes all those that he acknowledges as his sons. Suffering is part of your training" (Heb. 12:6-7). To attain the spiritual, internal strength and self-reliance are needed; dependency and rigidity suffocate growth. One's limiting concepts and emotional hangups have to be acknowledged, de-charged, and gradually left behind, just as "the things of a child" (1 Cor. 13:11) are left behind when one matures.

When his close disciples asked him, "What will be the sign of your coming and of the end of the world?" (Matt. 24:3), Jesus allegorically described to them the time of distress in spiritual practice that precedes liberation. But he assured them that this suffering was an intermediate and necessary phase, saying, "do not be alarmed, for this is something that must happen, but the end will not be yet. . . . All this is only the beginning of the birth pangs" (Matt. 24:6, 8). Then he instructed them in the way to deal with these difficulties. "Be on your guard," he said (Mark 13:9). "Set up in the Holy Place. . . . Stay awake because you do not know the day when your master is coming. . . . You must stand ready" (Matt. 24:15, 42, 44). Having established one's attention on the divine, one keeps it there constantly, cautious not to be drawn away by distractions ("temptations") of any kind.

Jesus then told his disciples, "When these things begin to take place, stand erect, hold your heads high, because your liberation is near at hand" (Luke 21:28). To attain liberation, one has to remain steady and straight, both mentally and physically. The Yoga Sutras also instruct the student to maintain a still and upright posture—both physically and mentally—during the practice of meditation. Patanjali views this as an essential aid in dealing with distractions and allowing one's consciousness to flow upward. The straight and steady seated posture of the yogic meditator keeps the spine erect and aligned, just as does the upright kneeling posture used by many Christians during prayer.

Jesus advised his students to be aware of the symptoms of progress that might otherwise alarm or mislead them and to understand "the signs of the times" (Luke 12:56). He cautioned them not to be swayed even by seemingly positive inner occurrences, saying, "False prophets will arise and produce signs and portents to deceive the elect, if that were possible. You must be on your guard. I have forewarned you of everything" (Mark 13:22-23). Finally, he admonished them to "Stay awake, praying at all times for the strength to survive all that is going to happen, and to stand with confidence before the Son of man" (Luke 21:36).

In counseling them in the ways to deal with the difficulties in meditative practice, he adjured them to always be alert and ready yet "not to prepare your defense" (Luke 21:14) nor to resist evil (Matt. 5:39). Defensiveness and resistance create tension and increase the flow of energy toward the negative, but a stance of total equanimity and disinterest in all but the divine focus helps one remain unaffected by potentially upsetting experiences. In the yogic tradition this is described as assuming the point of view of an objective witness throughout one's practice of meditation. One keeps one's focus on the divine and is not affected by or interested in any peripheral positive or negative stimuli.

Such a stance of equanimity and objective witnessing is essential to the meditative process. This method, called passive volition, allows the process of growth to take place as one systematically desensitizes oneself to anxiety-provoking internal stimuli. In this way, one allows the narrow repressive aspects of personality to fall away as one yields the defense mechanisms that protect the narrow ego. In a relaxed and focused state, one systematically desensitizes oneself to emotion-laden stimuli. Jesus fortified his disciples to persevere through these difficult times, saying, "When you see these things happening, know that the kingdom of God is near" (Luke 21:31). The obstacles and tribulations along the path are actually signs of progress that herald the advent of a new plateau—and ultimately of the pinnacle. The Second Coming and the Last Judgment that Jesus intimated referred not to his own return and leadership or to the demise of the planet but to the spiritual enlightenment each disciple was to experience upon fully realizing Christ-consciousness— the divine presence within.

Ascending and Descending Energies

Although there certainly are difficult periods during the process of spiritual development, Jesus assured his disciples that trust, yearning, and patience would yield the sought-after fruits.

Jesus encouraged practitioners to maintain their striving through all the difficult stages, saying, "The man who stands firm to the end will be saved" (Matt. 24:13), and "Your endurance will win you your lives" (Luke 21:19). He comforted them, saying, "There is no need to be afraid, little flock, for it has pleased your Father to give you the kingdom" (Luke 12:32).

Those who accept their selection to the path will be guided to the ultimate goal. Paul advised his students, "You can trust God not to let you be tried beyond your strength, and with any trial he will give you a way out of it and the strength to bear it" (1 Cor. 10:13). The self-therapy aspect of meditation also carries its own safeguard: only as much as one is capable of dealing with will arise. As one's capacity expands, so do the difficulties one must face. They become more subtle, more fundamental, and more deep-rooted, but, commensurately, one has acquired the ability to recognize and deal with them. This is the process of strengthening the *buddhi,* or discriminative intellect, which discerns the unreal from the real and guides one to Truth.

Buddhi also strengthens one's conviction and faith. Jesus said, "If you believe, you will receive whatever you ask for in prayer" (Matt. 21:22). If the inner storm becomes too wild, and the practitioner is frightened, he has only to call on the inner guide, as the apostles called on Jesus when they feared they would capsize. "We are going down!" they cried, and waked him. But he "rebuked the wind and said to the sea, 'Quiet now! Be calm!' And the wind dropped and all was calm again" (Mark 4:39). Faith, receptivity, and adamant desire warrant response. "To them that look shall he [the Father] appear" (John 14:23). The process is interactive. James counsels, "The nearer you go to God, the nearer he will come to you" (James 4:8). Having applied sincere effort to attain the ultimate goal, the goal itself begins to come toward the seeker and to pull the seeker toward it. As Pascal says of the divine, "If you search for me, you have found me." And St. Francis of Assisi states simply, "That which is seeking is that which is being sought." What the seeker is searching for is realization of his own essential nature.

The story of the prodigal son further describes the interactive process of growth between the seeker, who is aspiring upward, and the divinity, whose grace is descending from above. This philosophical concept is symbolized in the ladder of Jacob's dream (Gen. 28:12), and Jesus also describes heaven with "angels of God ascending and descending" (John 1:51). These two energies are depicted graphically in the two triangles of the Star of David, which design is also the *yantra,* or geometric representation, for the heart center in kundalini yoga. The symbol of the Christian cross demonstrates the same concept, with the crossbar at the heart center designating the juncture of the higher and lower energies. In Samkhya philosophy, which explains the theoretical paradigm of yoga, the ascending energy is called Prakriti and the descending is Purusha. In kundalini yoga they are referred to as Shakti and Shiva, and consciousness is said to travel upward through the chakras until the downward flow of grace dawns. The sign of the cross in the Catholic tradition delineates the chakras described in kundalini yoga and Tantra.

The union of the lower self with the higher Self is the purpose of all the meditative traditions of the world. The word *yoga,* meaning "yoke" or "union," refers to this, and Jesus told his students, "Shoulder my yoke and learn from me . . . and you will find rest for your souls. Yes, my yoke is easy" (Matt. 11:29-30). The teacher represents the higher Self, and when the individual self aspires upward, the teacher's grace, or *shakti pat,* is bestowed. The union of the individual self with the universal Self is the ultimate state, called heaven or Self-realization. Paul reports that Jesus "raised us up with him and made us sit with him in heavenly places" (Eph. 2:6). The uplifting of the lower self is possible through its striving and through the intervention of the spirit. Peter states that through God's gifts, "You will be able to share the divine nature and escape corruption in a world that is sunk in vice" (2 Peter 1:4). In yoga this is described as leaving the lower three centers of consciousness, which deal with issues related to security, sensuality, and power, and rising to the higher ones, which deal with compassion, appreciation of life, and wisdom. Attaining to the heart level is the first step beyond the lower animalistic levels; it is a transition to the human and heavenly centers of compassion, devotion, and wisdom that reside above the underworld ("hell") of fear, lust, and greed that the lower chakras embody.

The Power of the Word—Vak Shakti

In the meditative tradition of yoga, the link between the seeker and the sought prior to the experience of Self-realization is the mantra. A mantra is a subtle vibratory pattern that is experienced at the highest level of consciousness. It resonates with an aspect of divinity and thus guides the seeker through the turbulent waters of the unconscious mind to the mystical realm and beyond it. The Old Testament states the concept in this way: "He who walks in the darkness, to whom no light appears, let him trust in the name of Yahwey. Let him rely upon his God" (Isaiah 50:10). The name of the divinity and the divinity itself are synonymous, and the name is that which leads one from the darkness to the light. The Lord's Prayer states, "hallowed be Thy name" (Matt. 6:9), and John writes, "His commandments are these: that we believe in the name of his Son Jesus Christ and that we love one another" (1 John 3:23).

In the gospel of John, the importance of the word is emphasized greatly: "In the beginning was the Word: the Word was with God and the Word was God. . . . The Word was the true light that enlightens all men" (John 1:1, 9). The word is a mantra, the spiritual seed that manifests from the divine and that resides within the inner core of one's being. When nurtured, it stirs one to resonate with it until one's whole life is a representation of that divine vibration. Jesus made the Father's name known to his apostles "so that the love with which you [the Father] loved me may be in them, and so that I may be in them" (John 17:26).

The mantra is an inner guide that constantly directs those who attune themselves to it. Jesus said, "Listen, anyone who has ears to hear" (Mark 4:9); "Happy are . . . your ears because they hear" (Matt. 13:16); "He that is of God hears God's words" (John

8:47). Those who still their mental static can listen with their inner ear to the word of the silent voice within. This inner voice is the constant guide of the practitioner's life; it is that which imparts the teachings of the inner church. Jesus said, "The sheep follow because they know his [the shepherd's] voice. . . . they do not recognize the voice of strangers" (John 10:4-5). Those who turn within learn to discriminate between the voice of higher consciousness and that of the ego, the subconscious mind, and external influences. "The sheep that belong to me listen to my voice; I know them, and they follow me. I give them eternal life; they will never be lost and no one will ever steal them from me" (John 10:27-28). The mantra serves both as a guiding staff and as a shield, protecting the practitioner and leading him or her home. The practitioner follows the guidance of the divine vibration and becomes increasingly attuned to it—this is the prayer "without ceasing" referred to by Paul (1 Thess. 5:17).

The mantra emanates from a source beyond the realm of the mundane. Jesus said, "The word which ye hear is not mine but the Father's which sent me" (John 14:24). "I passed your [the Father's] word on to them. . . . I have made your name known to them" (John 17:14, 26); "The words that I speak unto you, they are spirit and they are life" (John 6:63). The "words" Jesus speaks of do not refer simply to his teachings but to this inner divine vibration or mantra, which is like a seed given by the enlightened teacher to the prepared student as a focus for spiritual practice—"The sower soweth the word" (Mark 4:14).

The mantra is a living thing that awakens the soul; likewise the word that Jesus conveyed was "the word of eternal life" (John 6:68). It was derived from the height of Self-realization, just as are the mantras that are conveyed to the student for meditation by the yoga master. Jesus said, "Heaven and earth will pass away, but my words will never pass away" (Luke 21:33); "My testimony is . . . valid because I know where I came from and where I am going" (John 8:14). From the vista of Christ-consciousness, all things past, present, and future are known, and the words given by such an accomplished sage are eternal living reflections of that state of divine perfection.

The use of the word, or mantra, as an aid in meditation is described by Paul. "The word of God is something alive and active: it cuts like any double-edged sword but more finely: it can slip through the place where the soul is divided from the spirit or joints from the marrow; it can judge the secret emotions and thoughts. No created thing can hide from him; everything is uncovered and open to the eyes of the one to whom we must give account of ourselves" (Heb. 4:12-13). The mantra sheds light on all the hidden aspects of the unconscious and dispels all obstacles impeding realization of the Truth. It cuts through all illusion and attachment down to the core of Truth, from which it emanates. Without the staff provided by such a divine vibration or mantra, the meditator soon finds himself or herself swayed by distractions and false influences. Mantra repetition, or *japa,* is an essential element of meditation in yoga, and it is practiced in Catholicism, also, in the Jesus Prayer and in the rosary (when practiced properly and in its simplest way).

In the yoga tradition, the power of the mantra, when used as a focus for concentration in meditation, is said to have the capacity to purify and transform the personality and lead the aspirant to experience the source from which the mantra emanates, the Ultimate Reality. Paul says, "He made her [the Church] clean by washing her with water with a form of words" (Eph. 5:26). Jesus told his disciples, "Now you are clean through the word which I have spoken to you" (John 15:3). In the science of mantra, the name of the deity is used to call up the character and power of that deity, for the name and the deity are one and the same. Thus Jesus instructed his followers to pray in his name (John 16:23-26) and to perform miracles in his name (Mark 9:39), and he told them that the Father would send the spirit to them in his name (John 14:26). The transformative power of the word is described in John: "To all who did accept him he gave power to become children of God, to all who believe in the name of him who was born not out of human stock . . . but of God himself" (John 1:12-13). And Peter told his students, "Your new birth was not from any mortal seed but from the everlasting word of the living and eternal God" (1 Peter 1:23). John recorded his Gospel so that "believing [in the divinity of Jesus] you may have life, through his name" (John 20:31). Jesus said, "Whoever keeps my word will never see death" (John 8:51). The word or mantra leads one from the mortality of body- and ego-consciousness to the immortality of spiritual awareness. It gives the eternal life of Self-realization.

The profound ability of subtle sound vibrations to manifest constitutes a philosophy and a science that is described in detail in the yogic scriptures, where it is called *Vak Shakti*. The Tantric concept of *Shabda Brahman*—the word as God—is conveyed in the Christian canon as well: "And the Word was made flesh, he lived among us" (John 1:14). Jesus was Logos, the Word incarnate. Thus, the mantra, the deity, and the enlightened teacher are inseparable, and when Jesus said "I am the Way" (John 14:6), that *I* refers to the divine word as well as to the teacher and the Lord. "Something has existed from the beginning that we have heard . . . and touched with our hands: the Word, who is life . . . that life was made visible" (1 John 1:1-2). The absolute essence of consciousness is this subtle vibratory pattern, which manifests outward to less subtle levels, thereby becoming energy and matter. In this way, the divine qualities of the sound of the mantra also eventually manifest into the material plane in the individual practitioner through its effect on the personality and behavior of that practitioner. Gradually, the person realizes that he or she is really a manifestation of the divine and ceases limiting this flow.

The word has the ability to bring balance and harmony where discord and disease exist. Mantras can also be used to render certain effects in the physical world. The Gospels indicate that Jesus "cast out spirits with a word and cured all who were sick" (Matt. 8:16). When he ordered a storm to cease, his apostles were amazed that "Even the winds and sea obey him" (Matt. 8:27).

Paul reports, "It is faith in that name [Jesus] that has restored this man to health" (Acts 3:16). The miracles that Jesus and his disciples performed are a demonstration that such phenomena are possible for those who are accomplished adepts. The third section of the Yoga Sutras describes these *siddhis* or special powers in detail. They are recognized as the natural outcomes or side effects of certain meditative practices and levels of consciousness. They make use of natural laws that science is only now becoming aware of but that yogis and great mystics have been utilizing volitionally for millennia. The application of such abilities often involves the use of a mantra. An obvious remnant of this phenomenon is seen in the Catholic mass when the priest breathes special words over the bread and wine to consecrate or transubstantiate them.

The mantra plays an essential role in the teacher/disciple relationship, as the teacher initiates the student by prescribing an individual seed mantra for his or her meditative practice. Further initiations and special practices (such as the *gayatri* mantra) are also given to students as they advance in their practice, and it is through such initiations that the tradition can be conveyed and the student evolve to the highest stage. When Jesus prayed among the twelve during his farewell discourse, he said to his Father, "I have made your name known to the men you took from the world to give me. . . . Keep those you have given me true to your name, so that they may be one like us. . . . Consecrate them in the truth; your word is truth" (John 17:6, 11, 17). The initiation, or baptism, that Jesus ordained was one of fire and Spirit (Matt. 3:11; John 1:33), and it was to be done "in the name of the Father and of the Son and of the Holy Spirit" (Matt. 28:19).

The parable of the sower explains the process of initiation and practice in this way: "The seed is the word of God" (Luke 8:11); "What the sower is sowing is the word" (Mark 4:14); "As for the part in the rich soil, this is people with a noble and generous heart who have heard the word and take it to themselves and yield a harvest through their perseverance" (Luke 8:15). The student accepts the seed mantra, which is a living essence of some aspect of divinity, and nurtures it in his or her heart so that it becomes strong, transforming and expanding the tiny ego into universal consciousness. Jesus said, "Happier are those who hear the word of God and keep it" (Luke 11:28). He told his disciples, "If you make my word your home you will indeed be my disciples. You will learn the truth, and the truth shall make you free" (John 8:31-32). The student must nurture the word and identify with it if it is to transform the personality and reveal the Truth. Jesus said, "If anyone loves me, he will keep my word, and my Father will love him, and we shall come to him and make our home with him. Those who do not love me do not keep my word" (John 14:23-24).

The word is the way to the Truth, and the teacher personifies the word because he has "listened to the word of God and acted on it" (Matt. 7:24). He is the manifestation of the word, and he gives it to his student. Thus, the bond between the teacher and the initiated student is special. Jesus said, "My mother and my brothers are those who hear the word of God and put it into practice" (Luke 8:21). The only true ties between people are spiritual ones, and the way to create this spiritual bond in the material world is through practice of the word. Constant inner awareness of the word or mantra is called meditation in action. "Never say or do anything except in the name of the Lord Jesus" (Col. 3:17). This ceaseless awareness of the divine is also characteristic of the yogic paths of service and devotion—karma and bhakti—which are the major routes that Jesus described.

Oneness with God

The transformation that occurs through turning within to the word "that enlightens all men" (John 1:9) is called Self-realization. This state of experiencing one's perfect union and oneness with the divine is the ultimate purpose and outcome of meditation, and Jesus was living evidence that this state is possible. The evangelists point out the oneness of Jesus and the divine frequently (e.g., 2 Cor. 5:19 and Luke 4:1), and Jesus himself also proclaimed this state of oneness: "The Father and I are one" (John

10:30); "The Father is in me and I in him" (John 10:38); "To have seen me is to have seen the Father" (John 14:9); "I came forth from the Father" (John 16:28); "I am not alone: the one who sent me is with me" (John 8:16); "Everything the Father has is mine" (John 16:15). Jesus acknowledged that he was the divine Christ, saying simply, "I am he" (John 4:26).

Jesus taught that realization of one's union with the divine was possible not only for himself but for his disciples as well. He quoted the teachings of the Psalms: "You are gods" (John 10:34, Ps. 82:6). And he prayed, "May they [the apostles] all be one. Father, may they be one in us, as you are in me and I am in you. . . . I have made your name known to them . . . so that I may be in them" (John 17:21, 26). He told his disciples, "He who eats my flesh and drinks my blood lives in me and I live in him" (John 6:56). He requested them to "make your home in me, as I make mine in you" (John 15:4). Before his departure, Jesus assured his followers, "I am with you always; yes, to the end of time" (Matt. 28:20). Jesus was called Emmanual, which means "God with us," and the highest school of Tantra—*samaya*—also means "I am with you." Its monistic philosophy describes a profound form of inner worship that views the body as the temple of the divine Indweller. The philosophy of Vedanta also regards individuals as temples of the all-pervading divinity, and Paul likewise affirms that each human being is a "temple of God" (1 Cor. 3:16) and that "the Spirit himself and our spirit bear united witness that we are children of God" (Rom. 8:16).

Jesus' philosophy seems to be in complete harmony with the monism of Advaita Vedanta—which states that there is only one Consciousness and that it is all-pervading, eternal, and un-changing—and Pauline philosophy is also in many ways similar to it. The statements Jesus made regarding divine union are comparable to the *mahavakyas,* or great statements, of the Upanishads: "There is only one Brahman without second. I am Brahman. All this is Brahman." The contemporary Christian Church does not share such Vedantic views, however, being dualistic and monotheistic, not monistic, in nature. The concept of unity was nonetheless the foundation of the early Church, and it remains today in the theory of the Mystical Body of Christ, which regards each individual as a cell in the corpus of divinity. Paul succinctly states, "You together are Christ's body" (1 Cor. 12:27). He explains, "We are all parts of one another. . . . Do all you can to preserve the unity of the Spirit by the peace that binds you together" (Eph. 4:25). John likewise states, "We are in union with one another. . . . We are in union with the Father and with his Son Jesus Christ" (1 John 1:7, 3); "God is love and anyone who lives in love lives in God, and God lives in him" (1 John 4:16). Paul continues, "May the peace of Christ reign in your hearts, because it is for this that you were called together as parts of one body" (Col. 3:15); "There is one Body, one Spirit. . . . There is one Lord . . . one God who is Father of all, over all, through all and within all" (Eph. 4:4-6); "There is only Christ: he is everything and he is in everything" (Col. 3:11). This reflects the same monistic concept as Swami Rama's comment, "There is only one God; that is all there is."

Self-realization is the experiential awareness of the divine unity pervading all existence, and the practice of meditation leads to this ultimate realization. The meditative tradition, as conveyed figuratively through the few words of Jesus in the New Testament or as described in the Yoga Sutras, the Upanishads, and the Bhagavad Gita, remains intact throughout various ages and cultures because meditation is both a basic human need and a natural state of being. Therefore regardless of the specific methods or philosophies used to attain or describe this state, human beings will continue to practice meditation and pursue its purpose. And, just as surely, great teachers and rare sages, like Jesus, who have evolved to the highest state will continue to appear from time to time to revive and reform the tradition and convey it to those who are eager to learn it and follow it to that same highest state.

References

Akhilananda, Swami. *Hindu View of Christ.* Boston: Branden Press Publishers, 1949.‾

Allegro, John. *The Dead Sea Scrolls.* New York: Penguin Books, 1956.

Arpita. "Jesus: Yogi for the West." *Dawn* Fall, 1981: 26-34.

Carpenter, Humphrey. *Jesus.* New York: Hill and Wang, 1980.

Goswami, Shyam Sundar. *Jesus Christ and Yoga.* London: L. N. Fowler & Co, n.d.

Graham, Dom Aelred. *Zen Catholicism.* New York: Harcourt, Brace & World, 1963.

Griffiths, Bede. *The Marriage of East and West.* Springfield, Ill.: Temple Gate Publishers, 1982.

Harold, Preston. *The Shining Stranger.* New York: Dodd, Mead & Co., 1967.

Jerusalem Bible. Garden City, New York: Doubleday & Company, 1966.

Johnston, William. *Silent Music: The Science of Meditation.* New York: Harper & Row, 1974.

Kelsey, Morton. *The Other Side of Silence: A Guide to Christian Meditation.* New York: Paulist Press, 1976.

King James Bible. New York: The World Publishing Company, n.d.

Leeming, Joseph. *Yoga and the Bible.* Punjab, India: Radha Soami Satsang Beas, 1963.

Maloney, George. *Prayer of the Heart.* Notre Dame, Ind.: Ave Maria Press, 1981.

Merton, Thomas. *Contemplative Prayer.* Garden City, New York: Image Books, 1971.

Needleman, Jacob. *Lost Christianity: A Journey of Rediscovery to the Center of Christian Experience.* New York: Bantam Books, 1980.

Notovich, Nicolas. *The Unknown Life of Jesus Christ.* New York: Gordon Press, 1963.

Pagles, Elaine. *The Gnostic Gospels.* New York: Vintage Books, 1979.

Panikkar, Raymond. *The Unknown Christ of Hinduism.* London: Darton, Longman & Todd, 1968.

Potter, Francis. *The Lost Years of Jesus Revealed.* Greenwich, Connecticut: Fawcett Publications, 1958.

Prabhavananda, Swami. *The Sermon on the Mount According to Vedanta.* New York: New American Library, 1963.

Prabhavananda, Swami, and Christopher Isherwood. *How to Know God: The Yoga Aphorisms of Patanjali.* New York: New American Library, 1953.

Radhakrishnan, S. *East and West: Some Reflections.* London: George Allen & Unwin, Ltd., 1955.

Sivananda, Swami. *Bhagavad Gita.* Durban, India: Sivananda Press, 1972.

Christian
Meditative Prayer

Sister Francis Borgia Rothluebber

I t is difficult to know what "meditation in Christianity" should encompass. Meditation, meditative prayer, is a very real part of living, in which we are on a search, a journey that is both a return and a leaving, that is moving to a future that we really do not understand, but that we welcome.

Meditative prayer has been an integral part of the Christian experience from the very beginning. We know that it was an important part of the life of Jesus: the movement to the desert, the movement to the mountains, or out to the ship on the water, was a very real part of his living; it was a breathing into his life. But, in a sense, we are concerned not only with those special times, those meditative, reflective times. We are concerned with the whole way of living, an approach to living. In fact, early in the Christian experience it was simply called "The Way": a way of living in relationship with the source of life, a universalized Jesus, who energizes and makes possible a rooting in reality that we could never, never know by ourselves.

This experience is the living of a parable. A parable is an answer that does not answer. It is always an answer that is both a challenge and an invitation. It is the paradox of living a truth in reverent tension, discovering a truth in reverent tension. It is losing one's life at the same time that one finds it. An emphasis on the Way, the Christian Way, that would be just losing one's life, would lead to a passive pathology. On the other hand, merely finding one's new life leads to a violent aggressiveness. We need the paradox of both the losing and the finding, the Paschal Mystery, the journey that is both dying and rising. This is the paradox to which we are invited in Christian meditative prayer.

This paradox, lived by the early Christian community and recorded in the Gospels, has been interpreted in a variety of ways across the ages. It would be an intriguing study sometime just to parallel the early Ignatius, who spoke of that water that kept drawing him to come to the Father, and the later Ignatius, whose whole approach to reflective prayer was carefully organized. Think of the differences between Teresa of Avila, Therese of Liseux, Juliana of Norwich, Francis of Assisi, Catherine of Siena, or Alfonsus Ligouri—such divergent approaches to reflective prayer in the Christian experience that it is difficult to get them encompassed into one approach. They are like facets, different ways this Gospel experience is interpreted in a given culture by a given personality.

It is difficult to talk about meditation. I think of Frederick Franck's account of opening a seminar with a very careful explanation of the Zen of Seeing/Drawing, and then deciding the only way was to go and do it. Go outside, sit down in front of that leaf. Look at it so quietly that it takes over and you can draw it without looking at the paper. That leaf has entered your reality. It is that entering reality, learning to breathe into your own life, that no one can lead you to. There are ways to help you start, but you must find, each of us must find that way of breathing that fits us; we must each find that way within which we savor life, we come more alive. It is something of this experience that I would like to share with you, both reflectively and in a kind of living it together, making it possible for you to enter something of such an experience.

Perhaps before we begin the experience, it would be helpful for you to understand that religious women in the United States— Roman Catholic, Anglican, or Lutheran religious women, Christian women—are on an exodus, responding to a call to move into a different way of living, a freedom and a searching that until now we have not known. Our foundresses began, generally, in the nineteenth century in Europe, and transferred to the United States the nineteenth century European approach to religious life for women.

Our congregations were generally organized to bring together a group of women who were interested in the immigrants who had come to the United States—women who wished to teach, women who wished to serve in health care or social service, women who were asked to build into their lives the contemplative, cloistered approach to silence. This included certain restrictions of travel and controlled scheduling of time with provision for work and prayer.

The question before us following Vatican II became: how can we minister to life so that we truly anoint it? How do we anoint life within us and around us? The answer was through healing. How do we utilize that healing experience of Jesus, that is ongoing today, in which the Spirit is being poured into us, anointing us, so that we can direct it outward to free others or to heal? To arrive at this answer, we have taken beginning steps in a new journey that we are finding more and more life-giving. They are old steps, but they are newly discovered. We find that we are learning that our meditative prayer is less a separation from life, as it was thought to be formerly, and more a stepping out of life to get a perspective on it—a dialoguing with our experiences, a dialoguing with life.

We need to approach the Christian message in a whole new light. In many ways we men and women have been masculinized by our experience in Western Christianity. The call for us is to incarnate those values that have been set aside in the process of masculinization—the values of interiority, of compassion, and of communion. These values are generally, in our society, looked upon as weak in contrast to the successful, more dominating approach of being first, having the most, or being "in control." Today we think of our reflective praying less as a prayerful person saying so many words, and more as a growing into our life, being more and more honest about who we are and what fits well within us, and what is leading us to greater freedom and greater energy.

We are learning that in a masculinized society the usual concepts of a woman's body carry negative overtones many women have interiorized, which must be rethought. We are rediscovering the sacredness of our bodies. We are learning to breathe more deeply, learning to take joy in our body, in the good sense of the body smiling. We are learning ways of becoming still, of quieting, of centering. As I work with young women today, I discover that they find even five quiet minutes very long, almost intolerable. We need to learn the way sound—sustained rhythmical sound—can help us to center ourselves. For most of us the symbolic, meaningful word is quieting and awakening.

I would invite you then to breathe deeply for just a moment, just to more fully taste the experience of breathing that many of you go through rapidly and quickly. I am going to begin a simple chant based on a phrase that is very present to me: "the tree." The tree is a significant part of our reflection at the early Easter season—especially the tree planted near living water, the tree rooted down into living water.

As you breathe more and more deeply, call out into your whole being that light from the tree. Let it flow out into you. Personally, and as humanity together here, we are that tree. We are sharing this life almost tangibly here. Let that life come up in us to energize us, to free us. And as the chant becomes familiar to you, come along, come with it, harmonize with it:

> Tree drawing light through its roots.
> Tree drawing light through its roots.
> Tree drawing light through its roots.

Into the quiet we read the word of scripture, from Isaiah 50:4, 5:

> The Lord Yahweh has given me a disciple's tongue. That I may know how to sustain the weary, he provides me with speech. Morning after morning he wakes me to hear, to listen like a disciple. The Lord Yahweh has opened my ear.

Everything depends on how we *read* the silence around us and within us. We are, Paul writes, a people seeking His face, groping, moving, knowing that in Him we live and move and have our being. We are learning that that which is yearning is not separated from that which is God, the Loving Presence who energizes us, who energizes our human life so that it comes to fullness in a faith relationship. We are learning to close the gap between natural and supernatural, human and divine.

As we breathe and reflect, we are entering more fully into the source of life that burns like a river of fire in each of us. We are learning that to come into touch with that river of fire means to come into our own reality. It means an openness to life, opening our hands, learning to open our whole being, letting our past come before us, owning and accepting our feelings, knowing how to examine in the Light that which is our fear, that which is blocking us, that which is disappointing us, that which is oppressing us, that which is giving us joy, that which is opening us to other people or to a new friendship—whatever the feelings are, to let them come into the Light.

Within that very experience sleeps the call that morning after morning we need to hear. Yesterday's word is not today's word, and we have not yet received tomorrow's word. Morning after morning we listen for the new word of this reality within which we live. The more we are in touch with the source of energy, the more freely we can walk hand in hand with risk, responding to the exodus call, being creative and being energized in ways we had not thought possible, drinking more and more of that living water that we have been promised, and that is here for our drinking.

We are learning to listen to the word that is in other's lives also—learning that the same source of energy that is within each of us is shared. There is one energy, so that we need not be in competition with other people. We need not seek to objectify, put people into boxes, or make them fit into roles. That same Life is calling out life in them, and the more the people with whom we live are energized, the more we are energized. We set up currents of support and currents of vitality, generative of all kinds of new ways of anointing life. The recent almost creative explosions that have been happening among religious persons are simply the beginnings of this kind of creative energizing.

Nothing wholesome and lasting can occur that is not grounded and rooted in interiority, in a nonviolence within oneself. At the same time, attentiveness and alertness move us toward making sound changes that can reshape human society. We are on a journey—I believe a very good journey. I know it to be good in my own life and I see it as good in the lives of other people. I am learning that it is not so much a question of the East and the West coming together as it is a question of what is human. What is fully human? Whenever we can discover what brings us to greater fullness of life, that is where our journey takes us. It is today that we are to be on that journey.

Let me conclude with a prose-poem story from the Talmud. Our Christian tradition flows in and out very closely with the Jewish tradition, and this story will illustrate what I have been trying to say:

About A.D. 250, the Rabbi Joshua Ben Levi met the prophet Elias. He asked him, "When will the Messiah finally come?" The prophet answered, "Go and ask him yourself." "But where can I find him?" asked the Rabbi. "He is sitting among the poor and the sick, and binding up wounds," said Elias. Rabbi Joshua Ben Levi then went to Rome, and there he found the Messiah, sitting at the gate, just as the prophet had described. He went to him and said, "Peace be with you, my Lord and Master." And he answered, "Peace be with you also, son of Levi." "When will my Lord finally come to redeem us?" asked the Rabbi. The answer was, "Today." Rabbi Joshua Ben Levi returned to the prophet and said to him bitterly, "The Messiah tricked me. He said he would come today. But he is still not here." To that the prophet replied, "So long as you don't know what 'today' means, he cannot come at all."

Yoga, Meditation, and Christianity

Pandit Usharbudh Arya, D.Litt.

Yoga, in the last few decades, has become a household word, and the practice of meditation has been gaining an increasing popularity. But in some quarters there are questions as to whether yoga and meditation fit with the doctrines of Christianity. Every now and then one encounters a certain amount of skepticism as to whether or not yoga meditation is compatible with Christian practices, especially among the very orthodox people of the West. This essay is therefore designed to help answer such questions as they relate to the meditative tradition in Christianity.

It must be remembered that Christianity, like all religions, has its roots in the East, so a study of the history of Christian doctrine should not be made in isolation from the history of general Eastern thought. Even though Christianity is today regarded as a distinctly Western doctrine, its Eastern orientation cannot be altogether suppressed. Christ still wears the robes of his land, and it is even possible that he might be denied entry into a modern hotel if he were to appear in downtown New York today.

Cultures develop strange prejudices and reactions to things that appear alien to them. Yet they cannot exist separately from each other, and a great deal of mutual appreciation and assimilation goes on unconsciously. No one in the West today, for instance, resents the use of the decimal or of Indian numerals. The use of calico and chintz was not discouraged because they were imported from India. Karate and judo are accepted as genuine sciences. Similarly, in the Eastern countries radio, tight pants, televison, and the necktie have become commonplace.

This type of mutual exchange among cultures has been going on for many thousands of years, including the period before and during the time of Christ. By the same token, even though it is Eastern in origin, meditation is not a non-Christian teaching; through meditation, true Christianity shares with the rest of the Eastern religions a seeking for God within and an aspiration to realize the true nature of the divine spark that is man.

If we look carefully at the history of ancient cultures we will find that such teachings continually flowed into the mainstream of early Christianity. One of the earliest examples of the Indian influence in Western philosophy, for instance, is to be found in the teaching of Pythagoras, who is regarded as the father of Greek philosophy. Then, if you read the fifteenth chapter of the *Metamorphoses* of Ovid, the famous Latin poet, you will find there Pythagoras' teachings concerning reincarnation, vege-tariansim, and meditational experiences—in verses that are almost identical to those of ancient Hindu scriptures. The reason for this is that Pythagoras, who rebelled against the tyranny of the rulers of his island, Samos, went eastward and studied there for many years before returning to Greece and establishing the first academy of philosophy in the West along patterns similar to those of an ancient *ashram*. The same rules of discipline and initiations were observed; the same philosophy of compassion toward all living beings was taught. And through Pythagoras these teachings spread to the West.

Such schools of philosophy, under the guidance of great teachers, continued throughout Greek history until they were closed by the orders of later Roman emperors. (It should be remembered that Pythagoras was a contemporary of the Buddha.) The philosophy of Socrates is thus recognized as bearing a strong resemblance to many of the teachings in the Upanishads. His emphasis on the incompleteness of sense experiences and on a higher reality behind appearances is nothing but the deepest Upanishadic philosophy. Once again, his dialogues on reincarnation, as well as his own personal life (as described by

Xenophon), bear testimony to some direct or indirect influence from the East.

Alexander of Macedonia, who conquered many countries and finally invaded northwestern India, was a disciple of Aristotle, who was in turn a disciple of Socrates. While Alexander was in India, he came into contact with Indian philosophers, and both Plutarch and Pliny referred to Alexander's contact with these sages of India and to the fact that he brought some of them back to the West with him. Plutarch, in his *Lives,* calls these philosophers "gymnosophists," but gymnosophists are none other than yogis, wise men who also practiced many physical exercises.

Then we come to the third century B.C., when the Emperor Ashoka ruled over a vast empire in India. Scholars have dug up inscriptions, known as the Edicts of Ashoka, declaring his philosophy and containing his advice to his subjects. These bear a marked resemblance to some of the teachings of Christ. That there was a cultural interchange between East and West is very possible because Ashoka exchanged ambassadors with the Ptolemies of Egypt and also sent Buddhist monks to establish monasteries in Syria. These Buddhist monasteries were still flourishing in the time of Christ.

Christ's mother tongue was Aramaic. Ashoka's inscriptions of three centuries before Christ were also in Aramaic, thus suggesting, on purely scholarly evidence, that the possibility of Christ's own contact with India cannot be ruled out.

In addition, many passages of the Old Testament are identical to those of the Upanishads. For example, God says to Moses that his name is "I am" or "I am that I am," which is the formula *soham,* used in many yoga meditations and found in the Vedas at approximately 3000 B.C. To consider another issue, who were the *magi* who visited Christ at his birth? Are they possibly the teachers of the doctrine of *maya* in Vedanta philosophy? The word cannot be explained in any other way.

The yogis of the Himalayas often say that Christ studied with them until the age of thirty, and there can be no argument with the fact that the baptism of Christ was identical to the initiations into the monastic life given among Buddhists and Hindus a thousand years before Christ. For three or four thousand years, as a matter of fact, monks of the swami orders have been introduced into monastic orders by taking a dip in the river, after which the initiating monk hands a rough robe to the new monk and blesses him by placing his hand on the initiate's head. The sentence in the Bible, "And the Holy Ghost descended like a dove" (John 1:32), and the present custom in the Christian church of ordaining a priest by the bishop's placing his hand on the new priest's head, are vestiges of ritual practices whose inner purpose is no longer understood. In yoga, however, such high initiations, whereby the guru's expanded consciousness is passed on to the disciple, are known and still alive in the Himalayan tradition.

The powers of yoga are so well known to the tradition of India that when the Hindu today reads the life story of Christ, his reaction to all the miracles described is that they are the *siddhis,* the spiritual accomplishments whereby the forces of nature are controlled. The miracle of walking on water is also mentioned in Buddhist scriptures. Many of the parables, such as that of the Prodigal Son, have also been traced to the same Buddhist texts.

In both the Jewish and the Western traditions, one stands to preach, whereas in the Buddhist and the Hindu traditions, a teacher sits. Christ sat to preach the Sermon on the Mount. Sentences like, "I am the Way and the Truth and the Life" seem to echo the statements of Krishna in the Bhagavad Gita. And long before St. John's Gospel the Sanskrit grammarians were writing of *Shabda-Brahman,* "the word that is God," for, according to the Vedic tradition, all Word was regarded as revelation; all teaching and inspiration as well as the whole universe originated from the principle of the mystic sound.

Saul, later St. Paul, on his way to Damascus, was not struck blind; he passed through a very high yogic initiation in which his eyes were closed by force so that he might see only the inner light.

It should also be remembered that some of the Christian meditative traditions have been traced back to Ethiopia and Egypt. Both countries had a continuous exchange of sages and mystics from India where the yoga philosophy had matured long before this time. Thus, the philosophy of the Upanishads and yoga continued to strengthen the mystic stream of Christianity long after Christ. Scholars have also established, without a doubt, that the neoplatonic school of Christianity owes a direct or indirect debt to the philosophy of the Upanishads.

In the Jewish tradition several sects followed disciplines that closely resembled those of the Hindu and Buddhist monasteries. What is more, the disciplines followed in the Roman Catholic monasteries today are very similar to those of the ancient Indian monasteries. Even though the dictionaries trace the origin of the word *monk* to the Greek *monos,* meaning "alone," I am of the opinion that its roots might go back to the Sanskrit *muni,* meaning "monk." The word muni occurs in this sense for the first time in a hymn in the *Rig-Veda* (1500 B.C.) in which the way of the lone hermits, who have withdrawn from the villages to forests and to a life of wandering, is extolled.

In this connection, observe also the following: the English word *man* has its origin in the Sanskrit verb root *man,* which means, "to think, to meditate." The Sanskrit *manas* is "mind" (Latin: *mens*), the instrument of thought and meditation. *Manu* is the first man, the first lawgiver, the personified *mantra.* Mantra (also manu) is a sound vibration introduced by a guru into the disciple's mind to make it a vehicle for meditation. Muni is a monk, hermit, or mendicant silently meditating with a mantra. *Mauna* is silence, the disposition of a muni. All of these words originate in the same root, which means, "to meditate." It is not possible that a monastic tradition could develop outside of the chain of concepts expressed by the single root *man.*

From the third century B.C. to the time of Christ, the trade between India and ancient Rome could not have failed to introduce Indian ideas of metaphysics along with silk, spices, ivory, and even some styles in sculpture. This trade continued through Byzantium and later through Venice. Is it possible that those who brought the decimal and the Indian numerals did not speak of the motivation of Indian life, the spiritual aspiration to unite with God?

Academicians have shown that *Aesop's Fables* and the stories of Andersen and the brothers Grimm owe their existence to the rich literature of India, especially to the *Panchatantra,* the *Jatakas,* and many other voluminous texts. The theme of the pound of flesh in *The Merchant of Venice* has been traced to the *Shivijataka,* one of the stories of the former lives of the Buddha. The story of *A Comedy of Errors* is in the same way a borrowing from a similar story found in the Sanskrit, *Ocean of Story (Katha-saritsagara).*

Some of the yoga doctrines became thoroughly distorted through this long journey from India to Elizabethan England. Take, for example, the fairies in *A Midsummer Night's Dream.* Shakespeare speaks of their homeland having been in India, and that they lived in flowers. Now, the word fairy is derived from the Iranian *pari,* which in turn is derived from the Sanskrit word *apsaras,* the celestial, semi-divine beings who gamboled on water at night, exactly the picture one has of the fairies from Shakespear's drama. The *devis,* divine mothers representing the forces of consciousness, reside in the lotuses of the *chakras,* the seven centers of consciousness according to yoga. They have no weight or volume, nor do the fairies, but a reader of *A Midsummer Night's Dream* today will not easily recognize this remote connection of the fairies with the chakras.

Now we come to the modern period. Goethe's praise of the Sanskrit drama, Schopenhauer's reinterpretation of the philosophy of the Upanishads (however pessimistic), Hegel's paraphrases of some of the Sankhya doctrine—all of these are enough to prove that the mystic philosophy of India was introduced into the West long before its recent renaissance.

The very foundations of American intellectualism are in Thoreau and Emerson, both avid readers of the Bhagavad Gita and the Upanishads. Emerson's concept of the Oversoul and his translation of some of the passages of the Upanishads are well known. His poem on Brahman, "If the red slayer thinks he slays and the slain thinks he is slain . . ." is a translation from the Bhagavad Gita and the *Katha Upanishad.* And Thoreau and

Emerson were not isolated thinkers. They were in the mainstream of transcendentalist writers of the time and were thus a strong influence on American culture.

We have given this historical outline in the attempt to show that what is being absorbed in American thought today from Eastern teachings is neither something completely new nor quite alien. The cultures of the East and the West have always borrowed from one another and will continue to. The present trend of bringing the spiritual teachings from the East to the West and the material sciences from the West to the East points to a very healthy future for our planet.

The meditative tradition has come to America not only via this East-to-West route, but also across the Pacific. This will be seen in the history of the word *zen*. The yoga word for meditation in Sanskrit is *dhyana*, which in Pali, the Buddha's spoken language, became *jhana*. The Indian Buddhist monks took the word to China, where it was pronounced *ch'an*. The Chinese and the Koreans then brought it to Japan where it became *zen*, and finally the Japanese sugar estate workers in Hawaii introduced it to California.

This journey of *dhyana* or *zen* from India to America took approximately two thousand years. It must be credited with having aroused a great deal of scientific curiosity in the United States, leading to the laboratory tests pioneered by men like Kamiya on the brainwaves of monks in meditation. Modern biofeedback techniques were the natural outcome of this.

The unfortunate part of the story of the spread of meditative philosophy in the West, however, is that it has, without fail, lost touch with its sources of grace and the original teachings, and each time a teacher comes he has to break fresh ground. It is for this reason that the West has never produced worthy successors to the masters of the Himalayas (except when some highly evolved Westerners make the Himalayas their home).

Each time a little bit of the teaching has been introduced, it has been mistaken for the whole, and the spiritually young have begun to play the guru. For instance, in Catholicism, the rosary and the repetition of prayer have been retained, but the higher consciousness of mantra has been lost. A small part of the Eastern healing technique, learned by Mesmer, became hypnotism (which is wrongly equated with meditation). Biofeedback research acknowledges scant debt to yoga in little footnotes because each researcher is anxious to proclaim the greatness of his own genius and "discovery." That would be perfectly all right if it did not fill people with false ego, which blocks the further flow of grace as well as the teachings from the great masters.

It should also be remembered that there is much in the history, doctrine, and practice of Christianity that is of the East, and more wisdom would have kept replenishing this reservoir if ego had not intervened and placed unnecessary obstacles in the way. For this reason all yoga meditation begins with the formula *gurubhyo namah,* "obeisance to the gurus: may their grace bless this meditation."

We have briefly referred to the similarities between the Bible and the Upanishads. These similarities can also be found in the later meditative stream of Christianity. The doctrine of apotheosis, for instance, reminds one of the Upanishadic passage, *Brahma veda brahmaiva bhavati:* "He who knows Brahman becomes Brahman." To be totally absorbed in one's deity, to lose the identity of the ego, to become one with the *ishta devata* (one's chosen deity), is an essential part of the Indian doctrine of *bhakti,* the path of emotional devotion to God. To a yogi of India, Christ can be one's chosen deity, and has been so with at least some of them.

What is the difference between meditation as practiced in Christian monasteries today and the yoga technique? Unfortunately, the depth of the yoga meditative tradition has been lost in these monasteries. The paths of an inward journey through the mazes of the mind into the deepset *sanctum sanctorum* of the divine heart have been forgotten. Mary is just a semi-human, semi-divine figure and no longer the Virgin Mother residing within all of us. Christ of the Sacred Heart exists only in icons and pictures.

Meditation as taught to an average Catholic monk is what a

yogi would term an act of contemplation. It is more in the nature of jnana yoga, the yoga of knowledge, in which a sentence of very high significance is taken, studied, examined, thought about, and absorbed into one's personality. But beyond such contemplation are the higher states of meditation, the levels of *samadhi,* in which such discursive thought and the words that are the vehicle of such thought are transcended, in which thinker, thinking, thought, and the vehicle of thought merge into one reality of supreme consciousness. This science of apotheosis, *Brahma-bhava,* has been lost and needs to be revived if Christianity is once again to become the source of inspiration that it once was.

What is the difference between the experiences of the Christian mystics and the yogis of the Himalayas? The narratives of the lives of Christian mystics indicate an emotional joy in union, and pain and crying and weeping when separated from the love of God. Such experiences come under the category of bhakti yoga, which is the uplifting of all emotions in surrender to the sublime. It is the yoga of the lover and the beloved. It is the song of the union of Radha and Krishna. It is the poem of the mystic-sage-poetess Meera, in the sixteenth century of India, and of the blind singer-saint-mystic Suradasa, who composed and sang ten thousand songs of devotion to Krishna. (It is said that the child Krishna would come and sit before Suradasa to listen to these offerings.)

A mystic's absorption in the joyful experience of God is the *samprajnata samadhi,* the meditation in which an object remains. Such a meditation may be accompanied with thoughts, with ecstacy, and one's own sense of separate self-existence. This is the case with the state attained by many mystics, both of India and the West. A yogi, however, is far beyond the state of being a mystic, for mysticism is only a step toward the highest samadhi (the experience of becoming one with the totality of the supreme consciousness of God). In such a state the expression of ecstasy known to the mystics no longer exists; these are left behind for the *bhaktas.*

Christianity is primarily a religion of bhakti, of total self-surrender, and it is this bhakti that appeals to the India of today to such an extent that no Indian of whatever faith can fail to cry when reading the Sermon on the Mount from the Gospel according to St. Matthew. But unfortunately, the Western Christian of today regards it as against his dignity to shed a tear in devotion and surrender. Instead, he splits the hairs of theology; he has changed the religion of bhakti into a religion of *jnana;* he has made religion an intellectual pursuit that examines doctrine with the thoroughness of a logician—but without making it a personal experience of God.

Those who are interested in true Christian meditation should understand the figures of the Mother Mary and the Christ of the Sacred Heart. The first steps in such a technique of Christian meditation would be as follows:

Perform a relaxation exercise in the corpse posture.

Sit up on your meditation seat, and after doing the basic breathing exercises and channel purification, visualize your *ishta devata,* the chosen deity: Mother Mary or Christ of the Sacred Heart.

Visualize this chosen deity in the space of the psychic heart, the cardiac plexus, or the depression above the stomach, below the chest, in the center.

The figure of your deity is radiant with light, sending out the rays of purest white divine light in all directions into your personality surrounding your own physical figure with the same aura of the purest white divine light.

Breathe slowly, gently and completely.

With each breath recite a prayer. If the figure is Mary, then recite "Hail Mary" with each exhalation and again with the inhalation.

If the figure is of Jesus, recite the name Jesus or some other brief prayer such as, "Lord Jesus Christ, have mercy upon my soul," "Hallowed be Thy name,""Let there be light,""I am that I am," or other such mantras. Some of the sentences may be divided into two, for exhalation and inhalation.

There should be no pause between the exhalation and inhalation.

Do not recite with your mouth, and do not move your tongue.

With each inhalation let the prayer go deep into your mind. Who is it that recites the prayer? Where is that divine spark from which all prayers are inspired? Go into the depths of your mind, holding onto the string of your breath, like entering into the depths of a cave in the center of which a divine spark burns.

Repeat the same prayer, and no other, at your meditation time and while walking, driving, sitting, cooking, having sexual intercourse, or falling asleep.

Do so until the prayer becomes a habit of your consciousness and it is remembered even when you faintly wake during your sleep.

When you have reached that point in your progress, ask your spiritual teacher for further instructions.

Whatever meditation you do, a spiritual instructor, a guru, is absolutely necessary. Those who have opened themselves up to *chit-shakti,* the Holy Ghost, have been graced with divine light and are the vehicles of this light; it is through their hands, their prayers, their grace, their saintly intercession, that the Holy Ghost descends into your soul. However, just about the time that Christianity was Romanized, it lost touch with its spiritual sources in the East, and as a result, grace and the blessings of the Holy Ghost through the gurus seems to have ceased. It is for this reason that even though a long chain of bishops has ordained hundreds of thousands of priests for hundreds of years, no divine experiences take place through these acts of ordaining.

The purpose of Christian meditation is, then, to realize a

unity of all personalities with the personality of Christ. The same also is the personality of Krishna or of any other divine incarnation. A reading of the ninth, tenth, and eleventh chapters of the Bhagavad Gita will greatly enhance the reader's understanding of the principle of this one divine personality of the universe.

In order to become true members of the Church of Christ a person must know not who Jesus was, but what Christ is. Christ, *Ishvara,* is the very personal force pervading this universe that guides and illuminates every aspirant. It is the very spirit of the guru. It is not an embodied person, but rather the force in which all individual beings are divine sparks, the *shakti* that has incarnated many times. As the consciousness of a finger is one with the consciousness of the person and cannot exist without that consciousness, without that unity, so the person also is a mere finger in the complete personality of Christ. It is in this way that he is a limb, a member of the spirit of Christ.

About the Authors

Swami Rama, the founder and spiritual head of the Himalayan International Institute of Yoga Science and Philosophy, was ordained a monk at a very young age by a great sage of the Himalayas. At one time he held the highest spiritual post in India, that of the Shankaracharya of Karvirpitham, which he renounced in 1952 in order to fulfill his mission in the West. He is the author of numerous books on all aspects of yoga. The Reverend Lawrence Bouldin is a minister of the United Methodist Church. Justin O'Brien, D.Th., the author of *Yoga and Christianity,* has taught at Loyola University of Chicago and has lectured at several other colleges. He is presently a faculty member of the Himalayan Institute. Father William Teska is a chaplain at the University of Minnesota Episcopal Center. Arpita, Ph.D., author of *Psychology of the Beatitudes,* is on the teaching staff of the Himalayan Institute where she also assists in the production of Institute publications. Sister Francis Borgia Rothluebber, former Mother General, School Sisters of St. Francis, is also past-president of the *National Catholic Reporter* and a leading author on religious life today. Pandit Usharbudh Arya, D.Litt., author of several books on meditation, is the founder and director of the Center for Higher Consciousness, in Minneapolis, and serves on the faculty of the Himalayan Institute. Dr. Arya is a former professor of Sanskrit and Indian religions at the University of Minnesota and a recipient of its Distinguished Teacher's Award.

The main building of the national headquarters, Honesdale, Pa.

The Himalayan Institute

The Himalayan International Institute of Yoga Science and Philosophy of the U.S.A. is a nonprofit organization devoted to the scientific and spiritual progress of modern humanity. Founded in 1971 by Sri Swami Rama, the Institute combines Western and Eastern teachings and techniques to develop educational, therapeutic, and research programs for serving people in today's world. The goals of the Institute are to teach meditational techniques for the growth of individuals and their society, to make known the harmonious view of world religions and philosophies, and to undertake scientific research for the benefit of humankind.

This challenging task is met by people of all ages, all walks of life, and all faiths who attend and participate in the Institute courses and seminars. These programs, which are given on a continuing basis, are designed in order that one may discover for oneself how to live more creatively. In the words of Swami Rama, "By being aware of one's own potential and abilities, one can become a perfect citizen, help the nation, and serve humanity."

The Institute has branch centers and affiliates throughout the United States. The 422-acre campus of the national headquarters, located in the Pocono Mountains of northeastern Pennsylvania, serves as the coordination center for all the Institute activities, which include a wide variety of innovative programs in education, research, and therapy, combining Eastern and Western approaches to self-awareness and self-directed change.

SEMINARS, LECTURES, WORKSHOPS, and CLASSES are available throughout the year, providing intensive training and experience in such topics as Superconscious Meditation, hatha yoga, philosophy, psychology, and various aspects of personal growth and holistic health. The *Himalayan News*, a free bimonthly publication, announces the current programs.

The RESIDENTIAL and SELF-TRANSFORMATION PROGRAMS provide training in the basic yoga disciplines— diet, ethical behavior, hatha yoga, and meditation. Students are also given guidance in a philosophy of living in a community environment.

The PROGRAM IN EASTERN STUDIES AND COM-PARATIVE PSYCHOLOGY is the first curriculum offered by an educational institution that provides a systematic synthesis of Western empirical sciences with Eastern introspective sciences using both practical and traditional approaches to education. The University of Scranton, by an agreement of affiliation with the Himalayan Institute, is prepared to grant credits for coursework in this program, and upon successful completion of the program awards a Master of Science degree.

The five-day STRESS MANAGEMENT/PHYSICAL FIT-NESS PROGRAM offers practical and individualized training that can be used to control the stress response. This includes biofeedback, relaxation skills, exercise, diet, breathing techniques, and meditation.

A yearly INTERNATIONAL CONGRESS, sponsored by the Institute, is devoted to the scientific and spiritual progress of modern humanity. Through lectures, workshops, seminars, and practical demonstrations, it provides a forum for professionals and lay people to share their knowledge and research.

The ELEANOR N. DANA RESEARCH LABORATORY is the psychophysiological laboratory of the Institute, specializing in research on breathing, meditation, holistic therapies, and stress and relaxed states. The laboratory is fully equipped for exercise stress testing and psychophysiological measurements, including brain waves, patterns of respiration, heart rate changes, and muscle tension. The staff investigates Eastern teachings through studies based on Western experimental techniques.

Himalayan Institute Publications

Living with the Himalayan Masters	Swami Rama
Lectures on Yoga	Swami Rama
A Practical Guide to Holistic Health	Swami Rama
Choosing a Path	Swami Rama
Inspired Thoughts of Swami Rama	Swami Rama
Freedom from the Bondage of Karma	Swami Rama
Book of Wisdom (Ishopanishad)	Swami Rama
Enlightenment Without God	Swami Rama
Life Here and Hereafter	Swami Rama
Marriage, Parenthood, and Enlightenment	Swami Rama
Emotion to Enlightenment	Swami Rama, Swami Ajaya
Science of Breath	Swami Rama, Rudolph Ballentine, M.D., Alan Hymes, M.D.
Yoga and Psychotherapy	Swami Rama, Rudolph Ballentine, M.D., Swami Ajaya
Superconscious Meditation	Usharbudh Arya, D.Litt.
Mantra and Meditation	Usharbudh Arya, D.Litt.
Philosophy of Hatha Yoga	Usharbudh Arya, D.Litt.
Meditation and the Art of Dying	Usharbudh Arya, D.Litt.
God	Usharbudh Arya, D.Litt.
Psychotherapy East and West: A Unifying Paradigm	Swami Ajaya, Ph.D.
Yoga Psychology	Swami Ajaya, Ph.D.
Foundations of Eastern and Western Psychology	Swami Ajaya (ed.)
Psychology East and West	Swami Ajaya (ed.)
Meditational Therapy	Swami Ajaya (ed.)
Diet and Nutrition	Rudolph Ballentine, M.D.
Joints and Glands Exercises	Rudolph Ballentine, M.D. (ed.)
Freedom from Stress	Phil Nuernberger, Ph.D.
Science Studies Yoga	James Funderburk, Ph.D.
Homeopathic Remedies	Drs. Anderson, Buegel, Chernin
Hatha Yoga Manual I	Samskrti and Veda
Hatha Yoga Manual II	Samskrti and Judith Franks
Seven Systems of Indian Philosophy	R. Tigunait, Ph.D.

Swami Rama of the Himalayas	L. K. Misra, Ph.D. (ed.)
Philosophy of Death and Dying	M. V. Kamath
Practical Vedanta of Swami Rama Tirtha	Brandt Dayton (ed.)
The Swami and Sam	Brandt Dayton
Psychology of the Beatitudes	Arpita, Ph.D.
Himalayan Mountain Cookery	Martha Ballentine
The Yoga Way Cookbook	Himalayan Institute
Inner Paths	Himalayan Institute
Meditation in Christianity	Himalayan Institute
Art and Science of Meditation	Himalayan Institute
Faces of Meditation	Himalayan Institute
Therapeutic Value of Yoga	Himalayan Institute
Chants from Eternity	Himalayan Institute
Thought for the Day	Himalayan Institute
Spiritual Diary	Himalayan Institute
Blank Books	Himalayan Institute

Write for a free mail order catalog describing all our publications.